GEORGE H.W.
BUSH

PRESIDENTIAL ✦ LEADERS

GEORGE H.W. BUSH

DIANA CHILDRESS

TWENTY-FIRST CENTURY BOOKS/MINNEAPOLIS

Twenty-First Century Books
A division of Lerner Publishing Group
241 First Avenue North
Minneapolis, MN 55401 U.S.A.

Website address: www.lernerbooks.com

Library of Congress Cataloging-in-Publication Data

Childress, Diana.
   George H. W. Bush / by Diana Childress.
     p.   cm. — (Presidential leaders)
   ISBN-13: 978–0–8225–1510–4 (lib. bdg. : alk. paper)
   ISBN-10: 0–8225–1510–5 (lib. bdg. : alk. paper)
    1. Bush, George, 1924– —Juvenile literature. 2. Presidents—United States—Biography—
Juvenile literature. I. Title. II. Series.
   E882.C48 2007
   973.928092—dc22   2005035739

Manufactured in the United States of America
1 2 3 4 5 6 – JR – 12 11 10 09 08 07

CONTENTS

George H. W. Bush accepts the Republican nomination for president at the Republican National Convention in August 1988.

INTRODUCTION

I seek the presidency to build a better America.
—George Bush, acceptance speech at the
Republican National Convention, 1988

In August 1988, the Republican Party met to nominate George Bush for president of the United States. The Democratic Party had already chosen Governor Michael Dukakis of Massachusetts as their candidate. The polls showed Dukakis far ahead of Bush. All eyes would be on Bush as he accepted his party's nomination. A truly great speech would help close the gap between him and Dukakis.

"I worried some about the speech and worked on it over and over again," George Bush wrote later. The press had been saying the speech would be "the biggest moment in my life."

When the moment finally came, Bush felt calm. "I knew what I had to do. I can't say that I was absolutely positive that it would be a 'home run,' but I was determined to do my best."

He began by praising the peace and prosperity of Ronald Reagan's eight years as president. "Now, after two great terms, a switch will be made," he said. "But when you have to change horses in midstream, doesn't it make sense to switch to one who's going the same way?"

His own philosophy, he said, centers on the individual, the family, and the community. "We are a nation of communities, tens of thousands of ethnic, religious, social, business, labor union, neighborhood, regional and other organizations, all of them varied, voluntary and unique." These communities are "a brilliant diversity spread like stars, like a thousand points of light in a broad and peaceful sky."

The crowd cheered the issues he promised to support: prayer and the Pledge of Allegiance in public schools, the right to bear arms, the death penalty, and antiabortion laws. He vowed not to increase taxes.

"The Congress will push me to raise taxes, and I'll say no. And they'll push, and I'll say no, and they'll push again. And all I can say to them is read my lips: No New Taxes."

The crowd waved flags and whooped with glee.

Bush described his dream for the United States: First-rate schools. A drug-free United States. Disabled Americans leading normal, active lives. A cleaner environment. Less dependence on foreign oil. More morality in American life.

He called for a "new harmony, a greater tolerance" among Americans. "I want a kinder and gentler nation," he said.

He closed with a promise. "I will keep America moving forward, always forward—for a better America, for an endless enduring dream and a thousand points of light." Then he asked everyone at the convention to join him in pledging allegiance to the United States flag.

The hall exploded with applause. Bush sensed that there was "something pretty special about it all." His fund-raiser

Bush speaks to the 1988 Republican National Convention.
This speech was considered one of his best. It caused a boisterous round
of applause and jump-started his presidential run.

Robert Mosbacher waved to Peggy Noonan, who had written the speech with Bush. "Out of the ball park!" he yelled. In the opinion of the presidential historian John Robert Greene, "It was the best speech of his political career."

Within days, the polls showed Bush inching ahead of Dukakis. Bush was closing the gap. He was on his way to becoming the forty-first president of the United States.

CHAPTER ONE

A PRIVILEGED CHILDHOOD

Our childhood was like a beautiful dream.
—Nancy Bush Ellis, younger sister of
George H. W. Bush, 1987 interview

George Herbert Walker Bush was born in Milton, Massachusetts, on June 12, 1924. His parents named him for his mother's father, George Herbert Walker. It was a long name for a baby, but his Walker family uncles soon came up with a nickname. They called their father, George Herbert Walker, Pop, so their nephew became Poppy.

Poppy was the second son of Prescott and Dorothy Walker Bush. He was two years younger than his brother, Prescott Jr. In 1926 a sister, Nancy, was born. Two more boys came along later: Jonathan in 1931 and William Trotter, nicknamed Bucky, in 1938.

When George was two, the family moved to Greenwich, a town in the southwestern corner of Connecticut near the New York border. From there, Prescott Bush commuted by train into New York City to work at an investment banking firm. His father-in-law was president of the company.

As the family grew, the Bushes moved to a large, rambling house on a tree-lined street. Set on two acres, the brown-shingled house had three stories and eight bedrooms. A wide porch wrapped around the house; a brook ran through the gardens in back.

A staff of servants helped out. There was a cook, one or two maids, and a man who worked in the garden, did repairs around the house, and drove Bush to the station and the children to school. Their comfortable lifestyle was not unusual among the wealthy families living in Greenwich. "We had a cook and a maid and a chauffeur," Jonathan Bush later told a reporter, "but other kids had a lot more."

———————————— ✧ ————————————

George was born in this house in Milton, Massachusetts, in 1924.

A CLOSE-KNIT FAMILY

The Bushes provided a loving, well-organized home for their children. "They believed in an old-fashioned way of bringing up a family—generous measures of both love and discipline," George Bush wrote later. Rules were strict, and standards were high. The boys wore jackets and ties at dinner. Inappropriate language was not tolerated. Honesty, modesty, and neatness were insisted on.

Religion played an important role. On weekday mornings, his mother and father read a lesson from the Bible before the

George, four, and his sister, Nancy (left), two

family ate breakfast together. On Sundays the family worshipped at Christ Church, an Episcopal church in Greenwich.

Both parents also encouraged sports. Dorothy Bush loved playing tennis and swimming with her children. She won footraces against her sons until the boys were well into their teens. Prescott Bush was an avid golfer who also swam and played tennis. The only excuse for missing church on Sunday was an important tennis match.

The two oldest boys were especially close. "Pres and George were as thick as thieves," sister Nancy later reported. "They were a twosome. Always shared the same room, and always together and shared friends." At one point, their mother decided it was time for each boy to have his own room. "That lasted for about two or three months," Prescott Jr. said in an interview. Then Christmas came. "Mother asked us what we wanted for Christmas, and we said all we wanted was a room together. So that was that."

SUMMERS IN MAINE

"We were a close, happy family," George Bush wrote in a memoir, "and never closer or happier than when we were crammed into the station wagon each summer—five kids, two dogs, with Mother driving—to visit Walker's Point in Kennebunkport, Maine." Walker's Point was a rocky ten-acre peninsula jutting out into the Atlantic near the mouth of the Kennebunk River. The spot was named for the Walker family, who bought it for a vacation home in 1901.

"Maine in the summer was the best of all possible adventures," Bush wrote. Along the shore, the boys played touch football in the sand or clambered over the rocks, pelting one another with the fruit of the beach plum bushes.

Going fishing with his grandfather, Bush wrote, "ranked right up there with eating ice cream and staying up late." Grandfather Walker used "the straight-and-simple method of fishing. Just a basic green line wrapped around a wooden rack with cloth from an old shirt or handkerchief used as a lure. Nothing fancy."

By the time George was nine, he and Pres had permission to take their grandfather's lobster boat, *Tomboy*, into the Atlantic by themselves. They learned how to deal with swift currents, waves, and tides, until "handling boats became second nature."

PRIVATE SCHOOL

George and Pres were so close that when Pres started school at the Greenwich Country Day School, George complained about being lonely at home. The following year, his parents enrolled him a year early, so that he began first grade when he was just five.

Prosperous Greenwich families had started the private elementary and junior high school to provide a full-day program for their sons. School for the 140 or so boys began at eight thirty and ended at six. The boys studied Latin, history, geography, mathematics, English, music, natural science, and art. The curriculum also included baseball, soccer, ice hockey, and swimming.

In the fall of 1937, George left home to attend Phillips Academy, a private high school for boys in Andover, Massachusetts. Andover, as the school is usually called, was founded in 1778. When George went there, it was one of the largest college preparatory or prep schools in the country. Its red-brick buildings spread over a fifty-acre campus.

George, thirteen, studies in his room at
Phillips Academy in Andover, Massachusetts.

Alongside dorms and classrooms stood a large library, an up-to-date science laboratory, and an art gallery with works by many famous artists.

Like the British schools on which it was modeled, Andover stressed Greek and Latin literature, history, mathematics, and athletics. Discipline was strict. Some called it "an academic boot camp." Most of the boys came from wealthy families, as the school offered few scholarships.

According to a classmate, George was only a "medium student." But he got along well with the other boys. His coach recalled, "Everybody liked the kid. He just had so much enthusiasm."

During his senior year, George came down with an infection that kept him hospitalized for weeks. "He came very close to losing his life before they were able to get it

George was captain of the baseball team during his last year at Andover.

✧ ————————————

under control," his brother Prescott said in an interview.

To make up for the lost study time, George repeated his senior year. The extra year in school gave him a chance to mature. He was finally the same age as his classmates, and he made his mark as a leader in sports and other activities. The Andover yearbook of 1942 has a long list of "Poppy" Bush's honors and achievements: class president, captain of the baseball and soccer teams, chairman of student deacons, deputy housemaster, varsity basketball player, member of the editorial board of the student newspaper, the *Phillipian*, and more.

ROMANCE

George was popular with the girls. His sister says, "He was sort of tall, and thin, and graceful, and handsome and funny. He was quick-witted and had a million friends." All of Nancy's girlfriends wanted to meet him.

During the Christmas holidays his senior year, George was at a dance at the Round Hill Country Club in Greenwich when he noticed a tall brunette with large, dark eyes. He asked a friend who she was.

"Want to meet her?" his friend asked

"That's the general idea," George replied.

Barbara Pierce lived in the nearby town of Rye, New York, just a few miles down the coast from Greenwich. She was sixteen and a student at Ashley Hall, a private boarding school for girls in Charleston, South Carolina.

As George's friend introduced them, the orchestra struck up a waltz. George did not know how to waltz, so he suggested they sit out the dance and talk. They hit it off so well, they never did get up to dance even when the music changed. The next night, they met again at another dance. After returning to their schools, the conversation continued in letters. Over spring break, George invited Barbara to be his date for his senior prom at Andover.

George's life, however, was changing. A few weeks before he met Barbara, on December 7, 1941, the Japanese bombed Pearl Harbor in Hawaii. The next day, the United States declared war on Japan. Germany and Italy, allies of Japan, responded by declaring war on the United States. Two broad oceans could no longer shelter Americans from World War II. George immediately decided that as soon as he graduated from Andover, he would join the navy to defend his country. Romance would have to wait.

Prescott Bush (1895–1972)

To his five children, Prescott Bush was "an imposing presence." His six-foot-four-inch frame towered over them. Prescott Bush was a living example of achievement and respectability. He expected his sons to measure up to his own high standards.

Born in Columbus, Ohio, to a well-to-do family, Prescott Bush attended an Episcopal boarding school in Rhode Island. Like his son George, he excelled in sports. He was a golf champion as a schoolboy and later played varsity baseball at Yale University.

At Yale he belonged to Skull and Bones, a secret society of fifteen seniors. He sang in the Yale Glee Club and with the Wiffenpoofs, a famous Yale singing group.

After college, Prescott Bush joined the army as an artillery captain. In 1917 the United

✧ ──────────
Prescott Bush stands proudly in his Yale baseball uniform around 1917.

States entered World War I (1914–1918) as an ally of Britain, France, and Russia against Germany and Austria-Hungary. Captain Bush saw action in northeastern France.

When the war ended, Prescott Bush went into business in Saint Louis, Missouri. There he met Dorothy Walker. The two married at her family's vacation home in Kennebunkport, Maine, in 1921. They settled in Greenwich, Connecticut, when Prescott began working at his father-in-law's bank.

After busy workdays in New York City and family dinners at home, Prescott Bush rushed out to civic meetings. For twenty years, he served on Greenwich's town council, most of those years as its moderator. He was active in his church, the local hospital, and charities. He also raised funds for the Republican Party. "Dad taught us about duty and service," George later said of his father.

In 1950 Prescott Bush entered politics. His first attempt to win a U.S. Senate seat failed. Two years later, his luck changed. He served for ten years in the Senate before he retired in 1962 due to ill health.

Prescott Bush died in 1972. George Bush wrote, "It was a real blow for me, for all his children. We had lost a best friend."

CHAPTER TWO

WAR HERO

*Although my childhood was very happy,
my upbringing was also strict—indeed,
puritanical. As a result, my vision of the world
was narrow, and I was a little judgmental at
age eighteen. Like most young people, my
horizon needed expanding.*

—George Bush, *All the Best, George Bush*, 1999

In early June 1942, Henry L. Stimson, U.S. Secretary of War, spoke at George Bush's graduation from Andover. He urged the young men to continue their studies in college. The war in Europe and the Pacific would last a long time, he said. With more education, they could serve their country better.

"George," Prescott Bush Sr. asked his son after the ceremony, "did the Secretary say anything to change your mind?"

"No, sir," he replied. "I'm going in."

On June 12, his eighteenth birthday, George Bush joined the navy as a seaman second class. "I was a scared, nervous kid," he said later.

TRAINING TO BE A PILOT

Bush was eager to learn to fly, and aviators were just what the U.S. Navy needed most. The Japanese had conquered the Philippines, Singapore, Indonesia, and numerous small island groups in the western Pacific. In 1942 the U.S. Navy began to slow the Japanese advance. For the first time in naval history, not ships but airplanes launched from aircraft carriers were winning the battles.

To get more pilots quickly, the navy no longer required that trainees have at least two years of college. It squeezed flight training into a rigorous ten months. Bush's flying lessons began in November at Wold-Chamberlain Naval Airfield in Minnesota. Through the winter, Bush flew in the bitter cold, wearing a sheepskin flight suit in the

————————————— ◇

Bush during his navy flight training in Minnesota

Bush sits in the cockpit of an Avenger bomber. Because he is left-handed, flying the plane was more difficult.

✧ ———————————

open cockpit. A leftie, he learned to work the joystick that controlled the plane with his right hand. He had to work hard, but he was determined. It helped that he loved flying. "Bush was an outstanding student," his instructor said.

Not all his time was spent in the air. At ground school, cadets at Wold also learned military history, physics, aerodynamics, Morse code, signal flags, and torpedo tactics.

In February 1943, Bush was off to Corpus Christi, Texas, to master three-point landings and advanced acrobatics. He practiced instrument flying on flight simulators and continued ground school. Three days before his nineteenth birthday, he earned his wings. He was the youngest pilot in the U.S. Navy.

PREPARING FOR COMBAT

More training lay ahead. Ensign Bush had to learn to fly the large-bellied torpedo bombers known as Avengers. The men called them "pregnant turkeys." He practiced taking off and landing on a short, narrow strip. Then came the biggest test: landing on a rolling deck at sea. Only the best pilots received assignments to aircraft carriers. Bush passed all the tests.

His reward was seventeen days' leave. He invited Barbara Pierce to visit him at Walker's Point. "We swam, rode bikes, played tennis, picnicked, walked in the moonlight—and fell in love!" Barbara said later. Secretly, they got engaged.

In September Bush reported to Norfolk, Virginia, to join torpedo squadron VT-51. He practiced aerial combat techniques and learned aerial photography. By January he was making landings on the USS *San Jacinto*, a new aircraft carrier. After a trial cruise to the Caribbean, the carrier set out for the Pacific.

AT WAR IN THE PACIFIC

Admiral Chester Nimitz's plan for victory in the Pacific involved "island hopping"—capturing strategic Japanese island bases to make stepping-stones toward Japan. By the summer of 1944, the United States had secured many outlying islands. A fleet of ships known as Task Force 58 was getting ready to break through the next barrier, the Northern Mariana Islands. In May the *San Jacinto* joined the fifteen other aircraft carriers in the task force. Battleships, cruisers, destroyers, and supply vessels supported the carriers.

The bombing of the Northern Mariana Islands began in June. Bush spent his twentieth birthday dropping four five-hundred-pound bombs on a communications center on the island of Saipan.

A week later, U.S. radar spotted more than four hundred Japanese planes swarming toward Task Force 58. The sky filled with white contrails (streaks) as U.S. fighter planes soared up to meet them.

To clear the deck for the fighters to take off and land, the nine bombers aboard the *San Jacinto* were catapulted off the carrier by slings like giant rubber bands. Soon after take-off, Bush's plane lost oil pressure. "We're going to have to ditch," Bush warned his two-man crew. "Prepare for a water landing." Aware that the landing might set off the bombs aboard the plane, Bush flew well away from the carriers. He set the plane down gingerly, tail first, on the choppy water. The three men quickly piled out. They rowed the life raft as fast as possible away from the sinking plane. Within minutes, the torpedoes on the plane exploded. Shock waves almost overturned the raft.

A nearby aircraft carrier rescued Bush and his crew as the battle raged overhead. By sundown, the largest air conflict of the Pacific War, the Battle of the Philippine Sea, had ended. U.S. planes had shot down hundreds of Japanese aircraft. Navy airmen called it "The Marianas Turkey Shoot."

CHICHI JIMA

The Japanese retreated to the Bonin Islands. From these rocky outposts six hundred miles from Tokyo, they harassed U.S. efforts to build airstrips in the Marianas. Bush's next assignment was to bomb Chichi Jima at the center of the Bonin island group. At the east end of the island, tall radio transmitters kept the Japanese navy informed of U.S. movements.

FLOATING AIRPORTS

The idea of floating airports began almost as soon as the dream of flight became a reality. The military wanted to be able to station bombers and fighter planes closer to their targets. In 1910 and 1911, Eugene Ely made the first airplane takeoffs and landings from ships equipped with wooden platforms built over their bows (the fronts of the ships).

In 1922 the U.S. Navy commissioned its first aircraft carrier, *Langley*, a converted coal-cargo ship. During the 1930s, the United States, Britain, and Japan built up fleets of aircraft carriers.

Carriers played a major role in World War II, especially in the Pacific. On December 7, 1941, the Japanese attacked Pearl Harbor with carrier-based planes. Six months later, the first naval battle in history fought almost entirely by airplanes occurred off Midway Island.

Takeoff and landing on a ship is tricky. As early as 1915, slings aided in getting planes airborne. Every carrier-based plane has a hook under the tail for landing. Several steel cables stretch across the flight deck. The incoming pilot "squats" the tail of his plane to catch one of the cables.

Aircraft carriers remain a cornerstone of U.S. forces at sea. The largest carriers in the U.S. Navy are the ten Nimitz-class carriers, named for Admiral Chester Nimitz. The tenth one is named the *George H. W. Bush*.

Rows of antiaircraft guns manned by Japan's best gunners surrounded the radio towers.

At seven fifteen on the morning of September 2, the
sling launched Bush's bomb-filled plane off the deck of
the *San Jacinto*. An hour later, the planes reached Chichi
Jima. As Bush dove toward the target, antiaircraft fire jarred
the plane.

"The FLAK was the heaviest I had ever flown into,"
Bush wrote later. "The sky was thick with angry black
clouds of exploding antiaircraft fire. . . . Suddenly there was
a jolt, as if a massive fist had crunched into the belly of the
plane. Smoke poured into the cockpit, and I could see
flames rippling across the crease of the wing, edging toward
the fuel tanks. I stayed with the dive, homed in on the target, unloaded our four 500-pound bombs, and pulled away,
headed for the sea."

"Hit the silk!" Bush called over the intercom to the
radioman and gunner. He received no response to his order
to parachute from the plane. Leveling the burning plane at
twenty-five hundred feet, he dove out onto the wing and
over the side. The tail section slammed into his head and
gouged a hole in his opening parachute. He fell rapidly but
remembered before plunging into the water to throw off
the harness that held the chute and the seat pack that held
a life raft and emergency supplies. Moments later, the
Avenger blew up in a "huge ball of fire."

Bush's crew was nowhere in sight. He spotted the yellow
life raft and swam toward it. He inflated the life raft, but
the paddles and emergency supplies were lost. He paddled
with his hands to keep the raft away from the island, where
he would be captured by the Japanese. For three hours, he

pulled against the current, his head pounding with pain. He was thirsty, sick, and burning hot. He wept for his crewmen and prayed for rescue.

At last, a small speck appeared in the water about one hundred yards away. "First a periscope, then a conning tower, then the hull of a submarine emerged from the depths," Bush wrote later. The USS *Finback*, assigned to lifeguard duty during the bombing, had spotted the downed flier.

ABOARD THE *FINBACK*

For the next month, Bush saw the war from a different point of view. The *Finback* did not have time to return the fliers it had rescued to their carriers. The submarine had orders to patrol the northern Philippine Sea for Japanese vessels supplying Chichi Jima.

Life was very different on a submarine. Bush got used to breathing the stale air, shaving with seawater, limiting

Bush is pulled aboard the Finback *by crew members on September 2, 1944.*

showers to one a week, and ducking as he walked through the narrow passageways. It seemed amazing to watch an air battle, as if it were a movie, through a periscope. Being attacked was another matter. Twice Japanese ships tried to sink the sub with depth-charges. "That experience was far scarier than an airplane bombing run," Bush recalled. "At least in the plane you controlled your destiny to some extent." In the submarine, "I felt trapped."

At night the *Finback* surfaced to recharge its batteries. Submarines at that time depended on electric motors powered by storage batteries while they were underwater. They rose to the surface at night and ran diesel engines until the batteries were recharged. Bush enjoyed standing watch on the *Finback* when it surfaced between midnight and four in the morning. "The nights were clear and the stars so bright you felt you could touch them," he wrote later. "There was peace, calm, beauty—God's therapy."

As he stood watch, Bush mourned the loss of his crew and other friends and pondered the meaning of his rescue. He realized how much his family and the values of his upbringing meant to him—and how much he loved Barbara.

BACK TO THE UNITED STATES

When Bush returned to his carrier, he flew more bombing missions over the Philippines. His flight group then received orders to return to the United States for a thirty-day leave.

It was a joyful reunion. Barbara met him at the Rye railroad station on Christmas Eve. They rode together to Greenwich, where his family waited to greet him. Twelve days later, on January 6, 1945, George Bush and Barbara Pierce were married.

George and Barbara Bush (third and fourth from left) *at their wedding surrounded by the Prescott Bush family* (from left), *Jonathan, Nancy, Prescott Sr., Dorothy, Prescott Jr., and his wife, Beth, and Bucky.*

◇

The young couple moved from base to base as Bush trained with a new torpedo squadron for his next assignment—the invasion of Japan. The war, however, was coming to an end. In May the Germans surrendered. Japan continued to fight until August, when the United States dropped atomic bombs on Hiroshima and Nagasaki. Then Japan agreed to an unconditional surrender on August 14.

In September George Bush left active duty. He had flown fifty-eight missions. For his "heroism and extraordinary achievement in aerial flight," the navy awarded him the Distinguished Flying Cross. He also earned the Air Medal with Gold Star, the Asiatic Campaign Medal with three battle stars, and the Victory and American Campaign medals.

The twenty-one-year-old war hero returned to the education interrupted by the war. He was off to college at Yale University. The "scared, nervous kid" had grown up.

CHAPTER THREE

FROM YALE TO TEXAS

My mind is in a turmoil. I want to do something of value and yet I want to and have to make money—after Georgie goes through 3 squares [square meals] every day, one's wallet becomes thin and worn.

—George Bush, letter to friend Gerry Bemiss,
June 1948

George Bush was not the only war hero at Yale that fall. Congress had passed legislation that paid education costs for veterans returning from the war. With the help of the G.I. Bill, as the legislation was popularly called, young men leaving the services crowded into colleges. The freshman class at Yale was the largest ever—more than eight thousand new students, most of them war veterans.

Like the other married veterans, Bush was "on a fast track to get my degree and make up for lost time." He studied hard. He enjoyed learning about economics, his major subject. His good grades won him the Francis Gordon Brown Prize for scholarship and character and membership in Phi Beta Kappa, the society for students with outstanding academic achievements.

Not all of Bush's time as a student was devoted to books. He joined a fraternity, led campus fund-raising drives, and took part in sports. "Technically my minor was sociology," he wrote later, but "my real minors . . . were soccer and baseball. Especially baseball."

✧ ————————————
Bush, like his father before him, played baseball at Yale.

SKULL AND BONES

During his senior year, George Bush was "tapped" for Skull and Bones, a secret society at Yale. His father had been a "Bones man" at Yale, and later his oldest son, George Walker Bush, also belonged to the club.

Formed in 1832, Skull and Bones is an ongoing tradition at Yale. Every year the fifteen graduating Bones members select, or "tap," fifteen upcoming seniors to become members. Their initiation and twice-weekly meetings take place in a windowless stone building on campus called the Tomb. When Bush was at Yale, Skull and Bones, like the university itself, accepted only men. Later, women were also invited to be members.

The motto of the club is *Memento mori*, meaning, "Remember that you must die." Skull and Bones focuses on the importance of lifetime friendships. At their meetings, the fifteen members form close bonds by telling one another their innermost thoughts. Members talk about their lives in detail.

Bones men from Bush's class of 1948 remember his moving account of his plane being shot down at Chichi Jima and the anguish he felt about losing his crew. One of the men

Married students such as the Bushes lived in large one-family houses converted into many small apartments. The young couples shared bathrooms and kitchen facilities. One of the houses where they lived had twenty-six adults and fourteen children crowded into it.

Barbara Bush had left Smith College in August 1944, after one year and one summer session. She chose to have a family instead of continuing her education. Their first killed, Lieutenant Junior Grade William G. White, had been a Bush family friend and a Bones man of 1942.

Membership in Skull and Bones lasts a lifetime. After graduation, Bones members retain close ties, helping one another out with emotional or financial support. Bones members from different classes also look out for one another. Neil Mallon, who gave Bush his first job after he graduated from Yale, was a Bones man in the class of 1917.

✧ ───────────
The Skull and Bones building (left) *is known as the Tomb because it has no windows.*

child, George Walker Bush (known as Georgie), was born in New Haven, Connecticut, on July 6, 1946.

When graduation loomed, Bush wondered what to do next. His biggest concern was supporting his family. He did not want to depend on his parents' help. Nor was he eager to work in his uncle's banking firm. "I was looking for a different kind of life, something challenging, outside the established mold."

Neil Mallon, a close family friend, had the answer: "What you need to do is head out to Texas and those oil fields. That's the place for ambitious young people these days."

LEARNING THE OIL BUSINESS

Neil Mallon not only gave advice, he offered a job. Mallon headed Dresser Industries, a company that makes tools for the oil and gas trades. He hired Bush as a trainee at Dresser-owned Ideco (short for International Derrick and Equipment Company) in Odessa, Texas.

Odessa introduced the Bush family to sandstorms, 105-degree heat, and the flat landscape of west Texas. The

———————— ✧
Bush (left) *spent time in the oil fields to learn all aspects of the oil business.*

working-class town was full of oil field laborers and oil supply salesmen. Bush put in twelve-hour days at work,
including Saturdays. He sold equipment, painted oil
pumps, even swept out the warehouse. Mallon wanted him
to learn the business from the bottom up.

In April 1949, Dresser transferred Bush to California.
For a while, he worked on the assembly line at Pacific
Pumps. He joined the United Steelworkers Union and
learned of the problems factory workers face. He felt sorry
for men who got laid off, he wrote a friend, but he believed
that layoffs are sometimes necessary. A business can't afford
to keep workers when the company isn't making enough
money to cover their salaries. "Business cannot survive if
labor is considered more than a 'cost.'"

That summer and fall, Bush sold drilling bits for Ideco.
Working out of his car, he drove "at least a thousand miles
a week." Barbara and Georgie moved around to be near
him. Near the end of the year, the family settled in
Compton, California. A daughter, Pauline Robinson Bush,
called Robin, arrived in December.

CATCHING THE FEVER
The following spring, the Bushes moved to Midland,
Texas, about twenty miles from Odessa. Many of their
neighbors were independent oilmen. John Overbey, who
lived across the street from the Bushes, became a good
friend. The two men talked for "hours on end" about oil
deals. Before long, Bush "caught the fever" and decided
that he, too, wanted to get in on the excitement. He quit
Dresser and with his neighbor founded Bush-Overbey Oil
Development.

The oil-rich land around Midland belonged to small ranchers and farmers. To find out who owned the land, Overbey and Bush "spent our time in the county court-houses," John Overbey said. They then convinced the landowners to sell their mineral rights. Other, larger companies did the actual drilling. If they found oil, Bush and Overbey stood to gain one-eighth of the profits. If the companies found no oil, only the farmer—who received money for selling the mineral rights—came out ahead.

For three years, Bush-Overbey "made a few good deals and a few bad ones," as John Overbey described it. It was a life "filled with risk and hope," Barbara Bush wrote later.

In 1953 Bush and Overbey teamed up with Hugh and William Liedtke to form a new company. By raising money from investors like Bush's uncle, Herbie Walker, the new business would have the capital to do its own drilling. They named the company Zapata Petroleum, after a movie then playing in Midland called *Viva Zapata!* It starred Marlon Brando as Emiliano Zapata, the peasant hero of the Mexican Revolution of 1910.

Just before Zapata's launch, the Bushes moved to a new house to fit their growing family. In February, John Ellis Bush was born. They called him Jeb.

A TRAGIC LOSS

A few weeks after Jeb's arrival, three-year-old Robin became listless and tired. Tests showed that she had leukemia, a cancer of the blood-producing organs. The Bushes' doctor told them that there was no cure for the disease.

Bush called his uncle, Dr. John Walker, for advice. Dr. Walker was a cancer specialist who was president of

THE BRIGHT STAR FOUNDATION

After their daughter Robin's death, George and Barbara Bush started a foundation for leukemia research in her memory. They called it the Bright Star Foundation. Since that time, new ways of treating this disease have developed, and childhood leukemia is among the most curable of childhood cancers.

Memorial Hospital in New York City. He urged the Bushes to bring Robin to New York. "You've got to give life a chance," he said.

For six months, the family watched and hoped. Barbara Bush remained at Robin's bedside in New York, while Bush flew back and forth to Texas. A former Bush family nanny went to Midland to care for Georgie and Jeb.

With blood transfusions and medications, Robin rallied. For brief spells, she did not seem sick at all. In August she was well enough for a visit to Maine. She even went home to Midland for a short stay. But she did not recover. In October 1953, she died with her parents by her side.

A TIME OF GROWTH

Zapata Petroleum, meanwhile, invested all its capital in one large field east of Midland. Every hole it drilled struck oil. By the end of two years, the company had 127 productive wells. The company invested in other properties in West Texas and set up Zapata Offshore to drill for oil in the Gulf of Mexico.

Bush's father helped make the new venture possible. As the senator from Connecticut, Prescott Bush led opposition to a bill to put all undersea mineral deposits within twelve miles of the coast under federal control. When the bill failed, private companies, such as Zapata Offshore, were free to drill in coastal waters.

The Bush family was also growing. Neil Mallon Bush was born in 1955, and Marvin Pierce Bush arrived in 1956. The family now lived in their dream house, complete with swimming pool.

✧ —————————
The Bush family (clockwise from top) in 1956— George H. W. holding Neil, Barbara holding Marvin, Jeb, and George W.

THE PULL OF POLITICS

As he got his start in the oil business, Bush thought often about entering politics. He was too busy to run for public office, but he was active in the Midland community. He taught Sunday school, coached Little League, and raised money for local charities.

When the World War II general Dwight D. Eisenhower ran for president on the Republican ticket in 1952 and 1956, George Bush led the campaign effort in Midland. Texas was a Democratic state. Republicans were so few, it was joked, they held their meetings in a phone booth. Texans, however, liked Eisenhower for his war leadership, his conservative views, and the fact that he was born in Texas. The trick, Bush learned, was to be sure that campaign materials did not have the word *Republican* anywhere on them. In both elections, Eisenhower carried the state.

His father's seat in the Senate showed Bush a darker side of politics. In 1956 the U.S. Senate began to debate a bill to remove federal controls on the price of natural gas. Texas oil and gas producers, Bush among them, favored this bill. Prescott Bush did not. Many oilmen asked Bush to urge his father to vote for the bill. Some even threatened not to do business with him if his father opposed the bill. The incident angered Bush, but it "didn't dampen my growing interest in going into politics."

CHAPTER FOUR

BITTEN BY THE BUG

The sun's going to shine in the Senate some day
George Bush is going to chase them liberals away.
—theme song of Bush's senatorial campaign, 1964

George Bush had always loved the sea. Drilling under the ocean promised vast new sources of oil. In 1959 Zapata split in two, and he took over the offshore part of the business. The Liedtke brothers kept the land operations. The Bushes moved nearer to the drilling rigs in the Gulf of Mexico.

They built a new home in Houston. It had "a pool, a small baseball field, trees to climb, and tires hung for all the children to swing on." They moved in with a new baby, Dorothy Walker Bush, nicknamed Doro.

The oil business kept Bush very busy. He flew to New York, London, The Netherlands, Mexico, Trinidad, and Kuwait to make oil deals. An employee quipped, "His name is George H. W. Bush—that H.W. stands for 'hard work' as far as I have observed!"

ENTERING POLITICS

Early in 1962, the chairman of the Republican Committee of Houston's Harris County moved away. Republican leaders asked Bush to run for the office. "This was the challenge I'd been waiting for—an opening into politics at the ground level, where it all starts," Bush wrote later.

Bush spent his evenings and weekends speaking to Republican groups, large and small, throughout the county. Barbara Bush took up needlepoint to survive the boredom of listening to the same speech over and over. The effort paid off. In February 1963, the committee elected Bush unanimously. For the next year, he worked to enlarge, enrich, and unify the Republican Party in Harris County.

——————————— ✧

George and Barbara Bush work hard on George's political campaign. A needlepoint that Barbara made adorns the bag in front of them.

State Republican leaders noticed Bush's energetic leadership. They urged him to run for the U.S. Senate in 1964. His opponent, Senator Ralph Yarborough, was a liberal Democrat. His voting record had angered many conservative Democrats in Texas, among them the U.S. president, Lyndon Baines Johnson. The time seemed ripe for a Republican to win Yarborough's seat.

Bush won the Republican primary in June 1964, but he faced an uphill battle. It was a presidential election year too, and Senator Barry Goldwater of Arizona was challenging President Johnson. Texans rallied behind their native son, Yarborough, and Johnson, putting aside his anger, endorsed him too.

During the summer of 1964, Bush crisscrossed Texas in the "Bandwagon for Bush." Barbara and son George, home for the summer before entering Yale University, campaigned too. With the slogan, "Bush is a Texan by choice, not by chance," Bush fought off accusations of being a carpetbagger—a Yankee trying to profit from southern politics. To win conservative votes, Bush promised to oppose labor unions, the Nuclear Test Ban Treaty, the admission of Communist China to the United Nations, Medicare, and even some civil rights laws.

In November, Johnson won a landslide victory. Yarborough rode in on his coattails. Although defeated, Bush captured more than a million votes in the election. It was the largest Republican vote in Texas history to that time.

TO WASHINGTON

Bush returned to the oil business after the 1964 elections. In 1965, however, "the political bug bit me once again." This

The Bush family (from left), Jeb, Marvin, George H. W., Doro, Barbara, Neil, and George W., at the U.S. Capitol in 1966. Bush's term as a representative from Texas began in January 1967.

——————— ✧

time, he focused all his energy on getting elected. He resigned from his official positions and sold his shares in Zapata Offshore. "I feel like I'm selling a baby," he wrote a friend.

He ran for the U.S. House of Representatives against a popular district attorney, whose views differed little from his own. He waged a handshaking "people-to-people" campaign.

Bush wooed black voters by backing a black girls' softball team. The team competed in the first integrated softball tournament in Houston. The "George Bush All Stars" won. And so did Bush. He was the first Republican representative from Harris County in the House of Representatives.

Arriving in Washington in January 1967, Bush gained a seat on the Ways and Means Committee. This important committee controls all bills that raise money to run the federal government. No freshman, or first-year, congressman had served on the committee in more than sixty years. The assignment was not just luck. Prescott Bush had left the Senate five years earlier, but many believe that his influence helped his son.

A TURBULENT TIME

George Bush served in Congress during a turbulent time. U.S. participation in the war in Vietnam (1957–1975)—which many people thought the United States had no business being involved in—and the battle for civil rights for

———————— ✧

Bush (right) helps load captured Vietcong rice in a camp near the Cambodian border during his trip to Vietnam in 1968.

African Americans made front-page news almost every day. Even a freshman congressman could not dodge these issues.

Bush supported the war in Vietnam. He listened politely to young people who came to his Washington office to protest U.S. presence there, but he did not change his views. In January 1968, he traveled to Vietnam to see for himself what was going on. He returned home convinced that U.S. troops were winning the war.

Bush's stance on civil rights, however, was shifting. In his race against Yarborough in 1964, he promised to oppose bills banning discrimination in housing. He argued then that the citizens of each state should decide what was right and fair for their state. In 1968 a civil rights bill with a provision that banned discrimination in housing came up for a vote. Bush held out against it at first. Letters opposing the bill swamped his office. But on the final vote, he changed his mind.

"Yesterday I voted for the civil rights bill," he wrote a friend who had urged him to support the bill. "Today, I am being fitted for my lead underwear. And Sunday, I go back to Houston."

Although he was joking about the need to wear bulletproof underwear for protection, Bush had reason to fear facing voters in Harris County. An angry crowd met him with catcalls and boos. When the people finally allowed him to speak, Bush reminded them that many African American soldiers were fighting and dying in Vietnam. "A man should not have a door slammed in his face because he is a Negro or speaks with a Latin American accent," he argued. Housing was not a handout or a gift, he said, but "a ray of hope" for minorities "locked out by habit and discrimination." At the end of his speech, he got a standing ovation.

Bush (right) supports presidential candidate Richard Nixon (center) at a campaign rally in Longview, Texas. Texas gubernatorial candidate Paul Eggers stands on the left.

A SECOND TERM

Bush was so popular that he ran unopposed that fall. He campaigned for Richard Nixon, who was running for president against the vice president, Hubert Humphrey. Nixon had considered Bush for vice president, but instead chose the more politically experienced Spiro Agnew, governor of Maryland.

During Bush's second term in Congress, he chaired the Republican Task Force on Earth Resources and Population. A strong supporter of family planning, he wrote the act that boosted government funding for family planning and population control.

A HARD DECISION

As the 1970 elections drew near, Bush faced a tough choice. Should he run again for the House? Or should he try once more to unseat Texas senator Ralph Yarborough? As a senator, he could have more influence than he had in the House of Representatives.

Bush's father urged him not to give up his seat in the House to run for the Senate. Bush decided to run anyway. As he showed with other choices he had faced—enlisting in the navy, becoming an independent oil operator, and entering politics—he was not afraid of risks. But Yarborough lost to Lloyd Bentsen in the Democratic primary. Now Bush faced an opponent who was almost a political twin. Both men were tall, handsome, well-to-do, and in their forties. Both were fighter pilots who had won medals in World War II. Both had built successful businesses and had served in Congress. Both were conservative.

The only contest between them was deciding who was more conservative, or farther to the right, in his beliefs. Bush was determined to take the most conservative stance possible. "If Bentsen is going to try to go to my right," he asserted, "he's gonna step off the edge of the Earth."

In the end, the few differences between the two men helped Bentsen. Bentsen had served one term longer in Congress, he was a native-born Texan, and most important, he was a Democrat. In a state where four out of five voters were registered Democrats, Bush was lucky to win 46.6 percent of the vote.

It was a crushing defeat for Bush. Comparing himself to the U.S. general who was defeated at the Battle of the Little Bighorn, he told a supporter, "I feel like Custer." He considered leaving politics.

Bush's daughter Doro was upset too. She burst into tears when she heard her father had lost. Her parents assured her that all would be okay. "Oh, no, it won't," she replied. "I'll be the only girl in the fifth grade whose Daddy doesn't have a job."

CHAPTER FIVE

HIGH-LEVEL APPOINTMENTS

Bush [has] talent, money, the background and inclination to do well in public life, and we ought to do what we [can] to help him along.
—President Richard Nixon, after the 1970 elections

In December 1970, as Bush was preparing to leave Congress, President Nixon invited him to the White House. He offered Bush an appointment as an assistant to the president. Bush accepted, but he also proposed another idea. Nixon needed a loyal supporter at the United Nations, he said. He and Barbara had many social contacts in New York City, where the UN headquarters was located. They could make friends for U.S. policies among the foreign delegates and for Nixon among the city's elite. Won over, Nixon offered him the job of U.S. ambassador to the UN.

Many people criticized the appointment. Bush lacked experience in foreign affairs and diplomacy, they said. Bush,

George H. W. Bush (third from left) is sworn in as U.S. ambassador to the United Nations. With him are (from left) U.S. Supreme Court justice Potter Stewart, Bush's wife Barbara, and President Richard Nixon.

however, remained optimistic. He said later that he saw two advantages. "First you have nowhere to go but up." Second, criticism "gets my competitive instincts going. They laid down a challenge, I was determined to prove them wrong."

UN AMBASSADOR

Bush focused on being a good host to the UN membership. He invited foreign delegates to family picnics at his parents' house in Greenwich, to boat rides around Manhattan, and to dinners at the ambassador's elegant Park Avenue apartment. "This week we took the ambassador of Madagascar to a hockey game with one of his boys and then Ambassador Ogbu of Nigeria brought his boy to go to a basketball game," he wrote in his diary. "I think this kind

of thing will be important to do, and I think it demon-
strates a certain friendliness that the UN ambassadors
should show to other people."

Bush found the social whirl tiring at times, but he used
it to get to know his colleagues better. Representatives such
as the Soviet Union's Jacov Malik, who angrily denounced
the United States at UN meetings, were friendlier, he
found, at dinner parties.

Barbara helped out. She learned the names of the representatives and their wives, found out what issues concerned
them, and introduced them to Bush at parties.

THE CHINA ISSUE

The major diplomatic issue Bush faced at the UN was the
question of Chinese representation. When fifty-one nations
met to form the UN in 1945, Jiang Jieshi (Chiang Kai-
shek) headed the Republic of China. In 1949, however, a
Communist revolution led by Mao Zedong drove Jiang's
government to the island of Taiwan.

For many years, Mao's People's Republic of China
appealed for admission to the UN. The United States,
however, argued that it was not the legal government of
China.

In 1971 the United States proposed a dual representation
policy. It would grant both Chinese governments seats in the
UN. Bush worked hard to find support for the policy.

That summer, news leaked out that Henry Kissinger,
the director of President Nixon's National Security Council,
was meeting with Mao. No one had told Bush about the
secret talks. He did not know if this meant that the United
States planned to change its China policy.

When the China issue came to a vote in October 1971, the People's Republic of China was granted the China seat in the UN. Witnesses saw tears on Bush's cheeks as he escorted the Taiwanese ambassador to the ambassador's car. Most humiliating for Bush was that, after the vote, many delegates danced in the aisles and jeered the United States.

Excluding a founding nation from the UN, Bush believed, set "a very dangerous precedent." The Taiwan-based Republic of China, he felt, represented many Chinese people.

When the new Chinese delegates arrived, however, Bush welcomed them. They made speeches hostile to the United States, but Bush followed U.S. State Department orders not to respond in kind. A new era of U.S.-Chinese relations was starting.

ENDINGS

In September 1972, Bush's father, Prescott Bush, fell ill. It turned out that he had an advanced case of lung cancer. His death on October 8 was a terrible blow. "My Dad was the real inspiration in my life," Bush wrote to President Nixon at the time. "He was strong and strict, full of decency and integrity; but he was also kind, understanding and full of humor."

That November, Richard Nixon was reelected president of the United States. At the first cabinet meeting after the election, Nixon aide Bob Haldeman told all cabinet members to turn in their resignations. Bush's appointment to the UN was over after only twenty-two months.

A NEW JOB

Bush had mixed feelings about leaving the United Nations. He enjoyed dealing with world leaders. But he also wanted to play a role in deciding foreign policy. He hoped that Nixon would make him assistant secretary of state.

Bush knew which job he did not want. Nixon was looking for a new chairman for the Republican National Committee. "Do anything but that!" Barbara begged him. As head of the Republican Party, Bush would have no role in international affairs or in government. It seemed a step down from his UN post.

Bush met with Nixon at Camp David, the presidential vacation retreat in Maryland, on November 20. The president told him, "The job I really want you to do . . . is over at the [Republican] National Committee running things." A national chairman oversees Republican Party activities in all fifty states, Puerto Rico, the U.S. Virgin Islands, Guam, and the District of Columbia.

———————— ✧ ————————

As chairman of the Republican National Committee, Bush (second from left) had meetings at the White House with President Nixon (center) and other key Republican politicians.

"You can't turn a President down," Bush told friends and family later. It was not just dogged loyalty. With his usual optimism, Bush looked forward to the challenge of improving the public image of party politics.

For Bush the new job meant traveling much of the time. The Bushes moved back to Washington from New York City. Only Doro and Neil were with them. Young George, Jeb, and Marvin were away at school.

NAVIGATING WATERGATE

Bush's appointment coincided with a major crisis for the Republican Party. In June 1972, during the presidential campaign, police caught five men breaking into the headquarters of the Democratic National Committee at the Watergate apartment complex in Washington, D.C. That fall the Federal Bureau of Investigation (FBI) proved that Nixon's Committee to Re-Elect the President (known as CREEP) was connected to the break-in. The so-called burglars had been installing listening devices to get information about Democratic Party plans. Many Americans were outraged at the idea of one political party spying on another.

Like many Republicans, Bush saw the incident as "the actions of a few misguided and very irresponsible individuals." He believed that Nixon was not involved in "the sordid Watergate affairs." The president is innocent until proven guilty, he argued.

In May 1973, a special prosecutor and the Senate began investigating the Watergate break-in. In July a White House secretary revealed that all conversations in the president's Oval Office were audiotaped. For twelve months, the White House refused to give the investigators the tapes from the time of the planning of the break-in. Bush defended Nixon's right to withhold the tapes. He said the president was protecting the privacy of sensitive information, not obstructing justice.

On July 24, 1974, the U.S. Supreme Court ordered Nixon to turn over the tapes to investigators. One of the tapes contained proof that Nixon had ordered a cover-up of CREEP's role in the break-in. When Bush and other cabinet members found out about the tape, Bush wrote to the president: "It is my considered judgment that you should now resign."

Nixon resigned on August 8. The next day, he left the White House and Vice President Gerald R. Ford took the presidential oath of office. It was a somber moment. Bush felt "saddened by what I saw as not merely a political disaster but a human tragedy."

✧ ——————————
President Richard Nixon sits next to transcripts of the Oval Office tapes shortly after telling the nation that he would hand them over to investigators.

SERVING PRESIDENT FORD

When Gerald Ford took over the presidency, suspense mounted over his choice for vice president. Many speculated that Bush was the front-runner. Instead, Ford chose former New York governor Nelson A. Rockefeller. Bush admitted to his friend James Baker that being passed over for the vice presidency was "an enormous personal disappointment."

Bush met with President Ford two days later to discuss Bush's future. Ford offered him a prestigious diplomatic position. Would he like to be ambassador to London or to Paris? Bush liked the idea of going overseas, but he wanted something different. How about China? Bush asked. To him, Beijing seemed more adventurous than London or Paris. It was "a challenge, a journey into the unknown," he wrote in his autobiography.

ENVOY TO CHINA

The People's Republic of China and the United States had not yet exchanged ambassadors and worked out full diplomatic relations. As head of the U.S. Liaison Office (USLO) in China, Bush would not be an ambassador, but he hoped to play a role in paving the way for future relations between the two countries.

Preparations began right away. Bush attended briefings at the State Department. Barbara packed and saw the younger children off to various U.S. schools and universities. Both studied Chinese. In October they set out.

The previous liaison officer had kept a low profile while the secretary of state negotiated with Chinese officials. Bush planned "to try to do more, make more contacts." He called on Chinese officials and invited them to dinner. He

George and Barbara Bush rode bicycles (above) around the city of Beijing during his time at the U.S. Liaison Office in China in 1974 and 1975.

———————————— ◇ ————————————

attended National Day celebrations at other foreign embassies in Beijing. At these events, he and Barbara met diplomats from other countries and many Chinese.

Eager to show the Chinese "that Americans are not stuffy, rich and formal," the Bushes joined the hordes of Chinese cyclists and pedaled around Beijing on Chinese-made Flying

Pigeon bicycles. On the Fourth of July—the first celebrated in Beijing since the Communists took over—Bush held a big picnic complete with hot dogs, soft drinks, and American beer.

Family, friends, members of Congress, and U.S. diplomats came to visit the Bushes. Bush introduced them to Chinese officials and businesspeople. He and Barbara and their guests toured Beijing and other Chinese cities.

Bush had little else to do. Secretary of State Henry Kissinger, who made three visits while Bush was at the USLO, tightly controlled the official talks. Bush had time to read and think about his future. He was having a wonderful time. But the political bug kept nibbling at him. By the fall of 1975, Bush was itching to go home.

A CALL BACK TO WASHINGTON

A telegram from Henry Kissinger came as a complete surprise. "The President asks that you consent to his nominating you as the new director of the Central Intelligence Agency," it read. It asked for "a most urgent response."

For Bush, the key words were "the President asks." "I accept," he cabled back. "Thank you for this honor. I will work my heart out."

Bush had many concerns about taking on the new job. For one, it promised to be "a political dead-end street." No director of the CIA could engage in politics while in office. He also worried that the Chinese would think that he had been a spy in their country and before that in the UN.

But the CIA desperately needed new leadership. Both the Senate and the House of Representatives were holding hearings on CIA operations. Many Americans were angry to learn that the CIA had ordered assassinations of foreign rulers,

Bush prepares to testify before the Senate Committee on Armed Services. This committee is in charge of confirming presidential appointments such as Bush's appointment as head of the CIA.

⸻ ◇ ⸻

overthrown foreign governments, and spied on antiwar groups in the United States. Heading the agency, Bush wrote his brothers and sister, "is perhaps the toughest job in government right now." He would have to steer a course between correcting "the abuses of the past" and standing up to "an effort to weaken our capability." Espionage is "not always a clean and lovely business [but] I am convinced it is important."

Bush returned to Washington to face Senate hearings for his confirmation in December 1975. It was the first time a president had named a politician to head the CIA.

Democrats and the press hammered away at the Bush appointment as "too political." Many senators thought that Bush would seek the vice presidency in 1976. To get his candidate approved, President Ford promised that he would not ask Bush to be his running mate. For the time being, Bush had to put aside his political ambitions.

DIRECTOR OF CENTRAL INTELLIGENCE

Bush threw himself into his new job with enthusiasm. Working twelve-hour days, he soon learned what he needed to know to run the agency. "He was a good listener," a senior analyst said in an interview.

He won the admiration of CIA employees by becoming one of them. Instead of directing the agency from Washington, D.C., he moved his office to CIA headquarters in Langley, Virginia. When a senior staff member asked, "Would you like to be called Mr. Director or Mr. Ambassador?" he replied, "Most people call me George." Everyone did.

He boosted CIA morale by naming a long-term agency officer, not an outsider, as his deputy. When he dismissed eleven of the top fourteen senior officers, he talked personally to each one. He then replaced them from within the agency.

At least once a week, Bush appeared before congressional committees. Often he brought CIA experts with him and let them present the testimony. Bush's leadership helped win approval of funds to improve the agency's technology. As a result, the CIA acquired two new satellite systems that could photograph through clouds and four new ground stations to intercept foreign communications.

Meanwhile, Bush kept away from politics. He did not attend the Republican National Convention in 1976 or help Ford in his race against Jimmy Carter. In November that year, Carter defeated Ford. President Carter did not want Bush at the CIA. On January 20, 1977, Bush became the first CIA director to leave office because of a change at the White House.

CHAPTER SIX

TAKING AIM AT THE PRESIDENCY

There's a certain luxury to beginning again.
I don't know for sure, but it's likely that
I'll save some time for politics.
—George Bush, leaving the CIA, January 1977

Bush returned to Houston to start a new life. For the first time since he graduated from college in 1948, he was truly jobless. With a Democratic president in the White House, he could not hope for the high-level posts he had enjoyed for the past six years. But many friends offered him work.

One of those friends was Texas billionaire H. Ross Perot. Would George Bush like to manage one of Perot's oil companies? Thank you, but no, Bush replied. "I have decided not to get back into the oil business," he explained. He also admitted, "I do not have politics out of my system."

Bush was eager to get back into politics. But he did not want to run for Texas governor in 1978. After the years in

Washington, in cabinet meetings, and dealing with foreign heads of state at the UN and in China, he aspired to higher office. He had just invited King Hussein I of Jordan to dinner at his new home in Houston. The only way to stay in the life he had grown used to was to aim for the White House itself.

BUSINESS INITIATIVES

Bush did not want a full-time job. He wanted to have time for politics too. But he needed income, so he became a consultant at the First International Bank in Houston. He also served on the board of directors of four companies. These businesses made little demand on his time but paid him generously.

Friends also proposed investment deals. When an associate started a business buying small barges to transport oil products, Bush invested in the company. His shares increased in value and provided him with a steady income. He also invested in an apartment complex.

With little work to do, Bush had time for community service. He co-taught a course at Houston's Rice University. He served on the board of directors of Baylor Medical College in Houston, his alma mater Phillips Academy in Andover, Massachusetts, and Trinity University in San Antonio. He also chaired the American Heart Fund and helped raise money for Yale University. These activities polished his image as a man concerned about giving back to society.

Bush also had time to travel. In the fall of 1977, the Chinese government invited the Bushes to return to Beijing. With a dozen friends, the Bushes toured China and Tibet. The next year, they traveled around the world. The trip included business meetings and political discussions with foreign leaders. They visited Denmark, Greece, Egypt, Israel, Jordan, Singapore, Australia, and Hong Kong.

GETTING BACK TO POLITICS

Bush traveled extensively within the United States too. Local Republican leaders, who knew him from when he led the Republican National Committee, invited him to give speeches. He raised funds and supported Republican candidates running for Congress in 1978. One of the candidates he spoke for was a freshman congressman, J. Danforth Quayle, who was running for reelection in Indiana.

To raise money for a Bush campaign, Bush's friends James Baker and Robert Mosbacher formed two political action committees. A political action committee is a group that raises and contributes money to candidates who are likely to support the group's interests. The Fund for Limited Government and the Congressional Leadership Committee helped other candidates as well, but most of the money went to Bush. These sources paid for Bush to "sky-hop" to forty-two states to make speeches.

The money also brought "some close friends"—members of Congress, businesspeople, and economists—to Kennebunkport that summer "to talk politics, issues, and my future." Between seaside clambakes and fishing jaunts, the group helped Bush plan his presidential campaign.

LAUNCHING A CAMPAIGN FOR PRESIDENT

In January 1979, Bush formed a presidential search committee. But there was no doubt in his mind that he was going to run. In May he declared his candidacy. He resigned from his consultant's job to devote himself entirely to the race.

The family joined in. Jeb left his job with a bank in Venezuela. Marvin, Neil, and Doro took leaves from their schools. Barbara prepared a slide show to introduce her husband to the American public. Bush's brothers and sister also worked for the campaign. Jeb's Mexican wife Columba addressed Latino voters in Spanish. Only George W., who had lost a race for the House the year before, could not leave his job to help out.

Bush was not alone on the campaign trail. Ronald Reagan, who had lost the Republican nomination to Gerald Ford in 1976, was back for another try. Governor of California and a former movie actor, Reagan had the support of conservative Republicans and Democrats. Bush found himself running with five other Republicans, all

Jeb Bush (left) *applauds his father's campaign speech. Neil Bush* (second from left) *and his fiancée, Sharon Hart, also attend the rally.*

elbowing for space as moderates, or those who take middle-of-the-road positions on political issues.

Bush's travel intensified. He spent 329 days on the road that year. "My feeling was and is that nothing beats personal eye-to-eye contact in a campaign," he wrote later; "not just talking to (or at) people, but listening to what they have to say."

In November the Republican Party held a statewide convention in Maine. Eight hundred delegates gathered. They listened to speeches by the presidential hopefuls and took a preliminary vote—a straw poll.

——————— ✧ ———————

Bush campaigns to be the Republican nominee for president in 1979.

Bush won the vote. Ronald Reagan, who did not attend, came in fourth. It was only a straw poll, not an official primary, but Bush knew he was starting to pull ahead of the pack.

CAUCUSES AND PRIMARIES

Election year 1980 began on January 20 with caucuses in Iowa. A caucus is a political party meeting to choose a candidate. Iowa's caucus is the first in the election season, and the winner there has the edge going into later caucuses and primary elections. Bush came in first in Iowa, capturing 31.5 percent of the votes. He surpassed Reagan, who ran second with 29.4 percent, and left the other candidates far behind. Bush's picture appeared on the cover of *Newsweek*. He no longer faced the problem of voters asking, "George Who?" Delighted by the win, Bush borrowed an expression that sportscasters used to describe a team on a winning streak. "We've got the momentum," he crowed. "Big Mo is on our side!"

The New Hampshire primary followed. Conservative newspapers derided Bush as a "spoon-fed little rich kid" and "an incompetent liberal masquerading as a conservative." This time, Reagan campaigned vigorously. His pep impressed voters who had worried that Reagan, at sixty-nine, was too old. On primary day, 50 percent of the voters chose Reagan. Bush received only 22.7 percent of the vote.

As winter turned to spring, Bush slogged on. But his campaign confused voters. Unlike Reagan, he defended the Equal Rights Amendment, which protected the rights of women and minorities, and opposed a constitutional amendment banning abortion. He called Reagan's plans to cut taxes without curbing federal spending "voodoo economics."

Yet like Reagan, he opposed federal laws to control gun ownership and defended capital punishment, which allowed the states to execute those convicted of murder.

News reporters had a hard time labeling Bush. Was he "a moderate in conservative clothing or a conservative with a moderate manner?" one asked.

Bush's speaking style didn't help. His thoughts often ran ahead of his words. As a result, his speeches were sometimes hard to understand. Reagan, on the other hand, knew how to present his ideas clearly and strongly. Newscasters nicknamed him the Great Communicator.

By the end of May, Reagan had won enough delegates to guarantee his nomination at the Republican National Convention. Bush hated to give up, but his campaign was deep in debt. He sent a telegram to Reagan congratulating him on his "superb campaign" and pledging "his wholehearted support in a united party effort to defeat Jimmy Carter."

THE CONVENTION

The Republican National Convention opened July 14 in Detroit, Michigan. Reagan had not yet chosen a vice president. Bush had his fingers crossed. He was, after all, the second most popular candidate. But rumor had it that Reagan was talking to Gerald Ford. Would the former president consent to be number two on the presidential ticket? Many believed it would be a "Dream Ticket," sure to unseat President Jimmy Carter.

As Bush headed to the podium to make a speech, a convention staffer shook his hand. "I'm sorry, Mr. Bush. I was pulling for you," he said. Reagan had chosen Ford, he explained.

In his speech, Bush released his delegates to vote for Reagan. When he returned to his hotel, Barbara and Jeb were packing to leave. Bush, however, refused to slip away. "We came to this convention to leave politics with style," he said, "and we are going to do it."

As they watched tele-vised coverage of the con-vention in their hotel suite, the phone rang.

A Reagan-Bush 1980 presidential campaign button

———— ✧ ————

"Hello, George. This is Ron Reagan," the familiar voice said. "I'd like to go over to the convention and announce that you're my choice for Vice President . . . if that's all right with you." Ford had turned down Reagan's offer.

"I'd be honored, Governor," Bush replied.

CHAPTER SEVEN

MR. VICE PRESIDENT

*I don't believe a President should have
to be looking over his shoulder wondering
if the Vice President was out there carving
him up or undermining his programs
in one way or another.*

—George Bush, in a letter to Richard Nixon,
January 12, 1982

In accepting Ronald Reagan's offer to run for vice president, George Bush knew that he had to embrace Reagan's political views. "If you are on my ticket," Reagan told him, "I expect you to support me on the issue of abortion." Bush agreed. His views on equal rights for women and "voodoo economics" also had to go. In his acceptance speech, he promised his "total dedication and energies" to promoting the party platform, the goals of the party that were worked out at the convention.

During the fall campaign, Bush kept his word and

maintained his loyalty to Reagan. If a reporter pressed him about how he differed from Reagan, Bush stressed their common ground.

In November the Reagan-Bush ticket won a solid victory. With 51 percent of the popular vote, the Republicans carried forty-four states. They also gained control of the Senate for the first time since 1952.

The Bushes sold their house in Houston and moved into the vice president's house in Washington. To avoid being left out of presidential decisions, Bush secured an office in the West Wing of the White House, near the president's Oval Office. He also arranged to meet with the president once a week and to receive all of the briefing papers sent to the president. With a newly hired staff of sixty-eight people, Bush set to work.

*This house is used by the vice president of the United States.
It sits on the grounds of the Naval Observatory in Washington, D.C.
Bush and his family lived here from 1981 until 1989.*

A HEARTBEAT AWAY

Bush soon showed how deeply his loyalty to Reagan ran. On March 30, 1981, President Reagan was just leaving a Washington hotel when shots rang out. A Secret Service agent pushed the wounded president into his waiting limousine, and he was rushed to the hospital.

Bush heard the news as he was flying to Texas to speak to the state legislature. Air Force Two, the vice president's plane, stopped in Austin only to refuel. On the way back to Washington, Bush arranged to meet with cabinet members at the White House.

When the plane landed at Andrews Air Force Base outside of Washington, a military aide advised Bush to take a helicopter to the White House. Bush refused. "Only the president lands on the South Lawn," he said. Instead, Bush went to the vice president's house and rode by car to the White House.

"The President is still President," he told cabinet members. "I'm here to sit in for him while he recuperates. But he's going to call the shots."

FIGHTING RED TAPE AND DRUG TRAFFICKING

During the campaign, Reagan had promised to "cut red tape, and get the government off the backs of the people." In February 1981, he had appointed Bush chairman of the Task Force on Regulatory Relief. For two and a half years, every department of the federal government worked to get rid of red tape (unnecessary regulations) that slowed down the business of the government.

Problems arose over some of the cuts. The head of the Environmental Protection Agency, Anne Gorsuch, dropped so many rules protecting the environment that environmental groups sued the government. The government lost the suit. Gorsuch resigned, and the regulations were restored. Because Gorsuch dropped the rules as a result of the work of Bush's task force, the incident hurt Bush's image with environmentalists.

Overall, the task force claimed success. Its August 1983 report said it had cut 600 million hours of paperwork and saved consumers, businesses, and government $100 billion.

In 1982 Reagan put Bush in charge of a task force to curb smuggling of illegal drugs into the United States. The program began in Florida. It later included other states. Under Bush's direction, the FBI, the Coast Guard, the U.S. Border Patrol, the Customs Service, and the Internal Revenue Service all took part. Arrests and prosecutions of drug traffickers rose, but the program did not stop the flow of narcotics into the United States.

WORLD TRAVELER

The vice president's job took Bush all over the world. For eight years, he stood in for Reagan at many events. Barbara Bush, who often went along, calculates that they clocked some 1.3 million miles together—the equivalent of fifty-four times around the world at the equator. Bush visited all fifty states, four U.S. territories, and seventy-three foreign countries as vice president.

Overseas travel was complicated. Planning began months in advance. Usually four airplanes made the trip. Air Force Two and a backup plane carried the vice president and about twenty staff members. Two cargo planes each carried a bulletproof limousine.

Vice President Bush waves from a tank in Nuremberg, West Germany, in 1983. He took many overseas trips as vice president.

Bush represented the United States at so many state funerals that people joked that Bush's motto was, "You die, I'll fly!" But it wasn't all ceremonial. These events gave Bush a chance to meet with other heads of state. Some of these talks were secret.

COVERT OPERATIONS

The Cold War between the United States and the Soviet Union was raging. Fighting Communism was an important part of Reagan's platform. Bush supported it wholeheartedly. One trouble spot was Central America. Communist-inspired rebels known as Sandinistas had overthrown the dictator in Nicaragua. They were also helping rebel fighters in neighboring El Salvador. To oppose them and their Communist-influenced government, the Reagan administration backed a group known as the Contras. Bush called the Contras Freedom Fighters.

Congress, however, voted against sending military aid to the Contras. Even so, the Reagan administration secretly began to help the Contras. In a deal with General Manuel Noriega, head of the Panama Defense Forces, U.S. secret agents used airfields in Panama to fly weapons to Central America.

The secret arms deals were not limited to Central America. In 1980 war had broken out between Iraq and Iran. Officially, the United States was neutral, but secretly, the Reagan administration allowed the sale of U.S. weapons to both sides. The goal was to prevent either side from winning the war.

Meanwhile, civil war in Lebanon led to the capture of seven Americans by Hezbollah, an Islamic terrorist group. Bush took part in cabinet discussions on how to rescue the hostages. Officially, the United States was opposed to dealing with terrorists. But secretly, the Reagan administration decided to ask Iran to persuade Hezbollah to release them. As part of the deal, administration officials offered to sell Iran weapons to use in its war against Iraq, even though weapons were also secretly being sent to Iraq.

Iran bought the weapons, but the plan did not succeed. Hezbollah released only a few hostages. Worse, they seized new American victims. The secret sale, however, illegally provided cash to buy weapons for the Contras.

In the fall of 1986, the web of secret deals with Iran, Iraq, and the Contras began to unravel. Over the next two years, information slowly became public as Congress and the courts investigated "Iraqgate" and the "Iran-Contra" scandal.

Bush denied knowing about the covert operations. Officially, he admitted that "mistakes were made"—without saying who made them. Later, in his autobiography, he defended the use of secrecy. "It's hard for people in a free society to accept the fact that covert action is often necessary for a world power to survive."

The closest Bush came to admitting publicly his own role was in an interview in 1988. When the newscaster Dan Rather pressed Bush about Iran-Contra, Bush referred to the torture inflicted on the hostages as the reason he "went along with it." He added, "If I erred, I erred on the side of trying to get those hostages out of there."

EYES ON THE PRESIDENCY

"I'm beginning to think a little in my heart of hearts of the Presidency," Bush wrote in his diary in July 1984. Preparations for the race began the following year. Bush chose a new campaign staff. He started raising funds and planning his campaign. Bush announced his candidacy in October 1987. His son George moved his family to Washington to help out.

Bush faced long odds. A sitting vice president had not won a presidential election since 1837. The press loved to poke fun at Bush's blundering speech. His polite manner earned him the label of wimp. One reporter even referred to him as "Reagan's lapdog."

A number of other Republicans challenged Bush in the primaries. In February 1988, the Iowa caucuses put him in third place. Undaunted, he headed for New Hampshire, where he gained a solid victory. Three weeks after that, sixteen states held primaries. Bush won them all. By April 26, when he won Pennsylvania, he had the nomination clinched.

Meanwhile, Democratic voters were choosing their candidate. The front-runner was Governor Michael Dukakis of Massachusetts. Americans were showing a great interest in

Bush campaigns for the presidency at a Medina, Ohio, rally in October 1988. His running mate was Dan Quayle.

the governor. A Gallup poll in May put Dukakis 16 percentage points ahead of Bush in the race for the presidency.

Bush spent the Memorial Day weekend with his aides in Maine. They told him he needed to speak more forcefully. And he had to attack Dukakis's positions. A "new Bush" emerged in June.

As the Republican convention approached, Bush looked around for a running mate. He wanted a fresh face, a promising candidate who would appeal to the younger generation. In a move that surprised even his staff, he chose James Danforth (Dan) Quayle, the forty-one-year-old senator from Indiana.

The confident "new Bush" and negative advertising aimed at Dukakis helped tip the balance to the Republicans in November. Bush won 54 percent of the popular vote and 426 electoral votes to 111 for Dukakis.

It was not a sweeping victory, however. Only slightly more than half (50.2 percent) of voting-age Americans went to the polls. It was the lowest voter turnout since 1924. Republicans lost seats in both houses of Congress.

George Bush is sworn in as president of the United States in front of the U.S. Capitol in Washington, D.C., on January 20, 1989.

CHAPTER EIGHT

MR. PRESIDENT

*I come before you and assume the
presidency at a moment rich with promise.
We live in a peaceful, prosperous time,
but we can make it better.*

—George Bush, inaugural address,
January 20, 1989

On January 20, 1989, George H. W. Bush took the oath to become the forty-first president of the United States. In his inaugural address, Bush radiated optimism. "A new breeze is blowing," he declared.

He called for a renewal of "high moral principle." Our goal, he said, is "to make kinder the face of the nation and gentler the face of the world." He asked Americans young and old to be less "enthralled with material things" and to reach out to help others in a "new activism, hands-on and involved, that gets the job done."

Bush also called for an end to partisan squabbling in

government. "The American people await action. They didn't
send us here to bicker."

Yet he knew many problems lay ahead. After eight
years of Reaganomics, Bush inherited a huge deficit in the
federal budget. A serious crisis loomed in the savings and
loan industry.

Worse still, the Democrats ruled Congress. Bush would
have to win their support for the United States he envisioned.

TANGLING WITH CONGRESS

Bush's first tangle with Congress came quickly. Bush chose
his loyal backer, Senator John Tower of Texas, to be his secretary of defense. Congress, however, balked.

The Senate Committee on Armed Services probed into
Tower's ties to defense contractors, his drinking habits, and
his affairs with women. The committee, controlled by
Democrats, did not recommend Tower for the post. Bush,
complaining of "vicious rumor and gossip," refused to withdraw the appointment. The Senate voted against Tower. It
was a big political setback for Bush.

More clashes with Congress followed. Bush proposed
changes for improving public education, curbing illegal
drugs, and reforming the welfare system, but Congress did
not act on them. Bush soon determined that his best
weapon in dealing with Congress was the presidential
veto. With his veto, he could reject outright a bill that
had been passed by Congress. With a threat to veto, he
could sometimes get Congress to modify a bill to make it
more acceptable to him. In his four years in office, he
used the veto forty-four times. Only once did Congress
override one of his vetoes.

SUCCESSFUL LEGISLATION

The president did sign some important laws. In August 1989, he signed a bill authorizing $120 billion to pay depositors who lost money when savings and loan banks failed. The bailout added to the huge federal deficit, but the new law put a stop to the kind of risky investments that had caused the bank failures and had hurt the industry.

Bush's vision of a "kinder and gentler nation" came true for disabled Americans. In July 1990, Bush signed the Americans with Disabilities Act. Some argued that the costs would hurt business, but many lawmakers from both parties supported the bill. Under the law, no one could discriminate against a person because of a handicap. Public buildings and transportation were required to become wheelchair accessible.

Bush also met his campaign promise to clean up the environment. In March 1989, the *Exxon Valdez*, an oil tanker, spilled 10 million gallons of oil into Alaska's Prince William

——————— ✧
President Bush
(center) *signs*
the Americans
with Disabilities
Act in the Rose
Garden of the
White House on
July 26, 1990.

Sound. The disaster and six-month cleanup rallied public support for stronger laws to protect the environment. In November 1990, Bush signed into law a major revision of the Clean Air Act. Hailed as landmark legislation, this law set air quality standards for all U.S. cities and reduced industrial emissions of pollutants.

THE BUDGET IMPASSE

Bush's worst struggle with Congress came with the budget of 1991, which was due October 1, 1990. The battle began in January. Bush proposed spending $1.23 trillion but added no new taxes. Just as Bush had described in his acceptance speech in 1988, Congress pushed for a tax hike. Negotiations stalled.

In that speech two years earlier, Bush had vowed that no matter how hard Congress pushed, he would say, "Read my lips: No New Taxes." But by the summer of 1990, Bush knew that the Democrat-led Congress would not pass his budget without new taxes. He would have to break his promise. When word leaked out, conservatives were furious. The headline of the *New York Post* ran, "Read My Lips: I Lied."

As the deadline neared, Bush's staff came up with a budget plan. To cover costs, it planned to raise the gasoline tax. Bush sent the budget to Congress at the end of September. He signed a resolution to keep the government going while Congress passed it.

But Congress voted down Bush's budget. An angry Bush refused to sign another extension. For three days, the federal government shut down. Tourists found national parks and federally funded museums throughout the country closed. People blamed Bush, not Congress.

It was a humiliating defeat. The budget Bush finally

signed raised income taxes for the richest Americans from 28 percent to 31.5 percent. Many Republicans believed Bush had betrayed them. Ten days later, on Election Day, the Republicans lost ten Senate seats, twenty-five House seats, and two governorships.

THE END OF THE COLD WAR

Bush was more successful with foreign affairs. His years at the United Nations, in China, at the CIA, and as vice president made him comfortable with world leaders. He knew many of them personally.

Major changes were taking place around the world. The United States' Cold War enemy, the Communist-led Soviet Union was weakening. For forty years, the two superpowers had dominated world politics. Nations allied themselves with either the Soviets or the United States. In 1989 these alliances began breaking up.

In Eastern Europe, countries rebelled against Soviet domination. The people of Poland, Hungary, East Germany, Czechoslovakia, Bulgaria, and Romania demanded democracy. Protesters knocked down the Berlin Wall, which had been built by East Germany to separate the Communist part of Berlin from the western section. Countries that had been forced to join the Soviet Union as republics also declared their independence from the central government in Moscow, Russia.

During the turmoil, Bush maintained good relations with the Soviet leader, Mikhail Gorbachev. Many Americans criticized Bush for not giving more support to nations opposing the Soviets. But Bush argued that stability was important. His strategy allowed the United States to make treaties with the Soviets to reduce Soviet arms and troops in Eastern European countries.

The Soviet Union finally collapsed. In December 1991, Gorbachev resigned. Eleven former Soviet republics formed the Commonwealth of Independent States.

CHINA

Bush took a similar approach in dealing with China. In April 1989, students began a massive protest against the government. For two months, they occupied Tiananmen Square in Beijing, demanding democracy in China. Their numbers grew, as more and more students and other citizens joined the demonstrations. On June 4, the Chinese government ended the protest by sending in tanks and troops against the unarmed civilians. Thousands were killed and injured, and thousands more were arrested and imprisoned. The United States condemned the Chinese government for the brutal crackdown.

——————————————— ✧

Bush met Chinese Communist leader Deng Xiaoping (right) when Bush was the U.S. liaison officer in China. He used his personal relationship with Deng to keep communication open during a difficult time—the Tiananmen Square uprisings in 1989.

Privately, Bush wrote to Chairman Deng Xiaoping. Bush urged him to be lenient with the students. With letters and secret talks, Bush kept communication open. By 1990 China was releasing students from prison to gain most favored nation trading status with the United States. (Most favored nation status meant that Chinese products exported to the United States would be subject only to the same tax rates that were paid by most countries that traded with the United States, not the higher rates paid at that time by many Communist countries.)

PANAMA

Another problem arose in Central America. During Reagan's presidency, the United States had paid General Manuel Noriega to aid the Contras. Noriega used the planes sent with supplies for the Contras to fly illegal drugs into the United States. U.S. courts indicted him for drug trafficking, but he remained outside the reach of U.S. law.

In 1989 the situation grew worse. Noriega seized control of Panama. In December Noriega's troops shot a U.S. soldier stationed in Panama. Bush decided the United States needed to protect the twelve thousand U.S. citizens living in that country and the Panama Canal Zone, an area on both sides of the canal that was controlled by the United States.

On December 20, U.S. troops invaded Panama. Noriega fled, and the U.S. Army put the elected government in power. Noriega surrendered January 3, 1990.

Although the invasion was successful, many Americans objected to Bush's actions. They argued that the invasion was illegal under international law. The Organization of American States and the United Nations agreed.

CHAPTER NINE

WAR IN KUWAIT,
BATTLES AT HOME

*Iraq will not be permitted to annex Kuwait.
That's not a threat, that's not a boast.
That's just the way it's going to be.*

—George Bush, address to joint session of
Congress, September 11, 1990

The following summer, a new crisis arose. On August 2, 1990, Iraq invaded its neighbor Kuwait. The Iraqi leader Saddam Hussein declared that the small, oil-rich country belonged to Iraq. This move gave Saddam Hussein control of 21 percent of the world's oil supply.

The UN Security Council quickly condemned the invasion. Bush telephoned leaders around the world. He urged them to take united action against Iraq. Within days, the UN Security Council voted to bar trade with Iraq.

Meanwhile, U.S. intelligence reported Iraqi troops on the border of Saudi Arabia. Bush warned the Saudi king

Fahd that Saddam Hussein planned to invade Fahd's country. King Fahd agreed to allow U.S. troops to enter Saudi Arabia to defend the country from attack.

DESERT SHIELD

The first U.S. soldiers of Operation Desert Shield, as the protective force was called, landed August 7. Several member countries of the League of Arab States, among them Bahrain, Qatar, Oman, United Arab Emirates, Egypt, and Syria, soon joined King Fahd against Saddam Hussein. Some sent troops to protect Saudi Arabia from invasion.

"A line has been drawn in the sand," Bush told Americans on August 8. He called for "the immediate, unconditional, and complete withdrawal of all Iraqi forces

——————————— ✧ ———————————

Bush (center) *walks with his wife, Barbara* (left), *and General Norman Schwarzkopf* (right) *through the Saudi Arabian desert in November 1990.*

from Kuwait." Americans praised his skillful response to the crisis. Bush's approval ratings soared.

Many countries hoped that the UN-sponsored trade ban would force Saddam Hussein to back down. Instead, he dug in. Bush knew that war might be necessary. As the summer drew to a close, he called up more troops.

During the fall, the UN Security Council passed more resolutions condemning Iraq's actions. Bush, however, saw his popularity dropping as Americans debated the need for U.S. troops in the Middle East. Antiwar protesters chanted, "No blood for oil." Democrats warned of a quagmire (a hard-to-escape trap).

On November 29, the UN Security Council set a deadline for Iraq to withdraw from Kuwait: January 15, 1991. Bush had lined up twelve Security Council resolutions and a coalition of twenty-eight countries to enforce the resolutions. He maintained that he did not need approval from Congress to take U.S. troops into war. After the Vietnam War, Congress had passed the War Powers Resolution, which required congressional approval for military actions in a hostile area, but Bush believed that law was unconstitutional. Even so, he wanted political backing from Congress to prevent protests from U.S. citizens who disagreed with him. On January 12, Congress voted to support the UN resolutions.

DESERT STORM

On January 15, President Bush ordered air strikes against Iraq to begin the next night. "Oh God, give me the strength to do what is right," he wrote in his diary.

Once the war began, Bush trusted the military to run it. Secretary of Defense Richard Cheney, Chairman of the

Bush (seated at desk) *speaks with British Prime Minister John Major while Colin Powell* (left) *speaks with Norman Schwarzkopf in the Oval Office of the White House during Operation Desert Storm (February 27, 1991).*

————————————— ✧ —————————————

Joint Chiefs of Staff Colin Powell, and General Norman Schwarzkopf were in charge.

Americans followed the war closely on television. The Cable News Network (CNN), with Peter Arnett reporting from Baghdad, provided twenty-four-hour a day coverage.

After six weeks of punishing air strikes, the ground war began February 24, 1991. Within four days, the Iraqi army was fleeing back to Iraq or surrendering to coalition forces. Our mission has been accomplished, Powell told Bush at his briefing the morning of February 27. "Why not end it today?" Bush asked.

President Bush speaks to a joint session of Congress on
March 6, 1991, about the end of the war with Iraq.

———————————— ◇ ————————————

Americans were relieved that the war was over. U.S. casualties were low—148 troops killed and 458 wounded. Bush's popularity soared. On March 6, he addressed a joint session of Congress and declared, "Kuwait is free!" Many Americans praised Bush for leading a successful international mission against unlawful aggression.

A ONE-TERM PRESIDENT

Bush's approval rating sank after the Persian Gulf War ended. He again faced battles with Congress. They argued over the budget. They disagreed over civil rights and affirmative action measures designed to give minorities preferred treatment in jobs and higher education. And

Congress questioned Bush's nomination of Clarence Thomas to the Supreme Court to replace retiring Justice Thurgood Marshall.

The Thomas appointment was especially damaging to Bush. In televised hearings, many Republican senators challenged law professor Anita Hill when she accused Thomas of sexually harassing her during his tenure as head of the Equal Employment Opportunity Commission. Their attempt to discredit Hill by not taking her accusations seriously angered many women voters.

In the end, Bush signed a new Civil Rights Act, and the Senate narrowly approved Thomas's appointment, 52–48. But the president was losing many supporters.

An even worse problem for Bush was the economy. A recession had begun in the summer of 1990. By early 1991, the major automakers were closing plants and laying off workers. Large corporations were firing middle managers (office workers who weren't top executives), a process they called downsizing. In June 1991, the national unemployment rate hit an eight-year high of 7.8 percent. Nevertheless, in September, Bush vetoed a bill that would extend benefits for the unemployed.

As the 1992 election approached, candidates hoping to unseat Bush focused on money and jobs. Patrick J. Buchanan, a conservative journalist, challenged Bush in the Republican primaries. H. Ross Perot, the Texas billionaire who once offered Bush a job, entered the race as an independent (someone without the backing of one of the two major political parties). Both Buchanan and Perot attacked Bush's reversal on taxes. They also opposed his support of tax-free trade with Mexico and Canada. The proposed

North American Free Trade Agreement (NAFTA), they claimed, would hurt U.S. industry.

The Democratic presidential candidate was Governor Bill Clinton of Arkansas. The Clinton campaign came up with a slogan that most voters agreed with: "It's the economy, stupid!"

Bush hoped that the economy would improve. It did. Economic signposts began to rise in April 1992. But it was too late to help Bush. He was running a lackluster campaign. Often he seemed tired of it all. He even glanced at his watch during a presidential debate. His health was

✧ ————————

Bush and his mother, Dorothy Walker Bush, at Walker's Point, Kennebunkport, Maine

another obstacle. He had a heart problem caused by Graves' disease, a kidney disease. The medications for it slowed him down. In his diary, he often said that he wouldn't mind retiring. "Great happiness lies out there if indeed the voters just say 'no,'" he wrote in early 1992.

Even though Buchanan lost in the primaries, conservatives contributed heavily to Buchanan's campaign, which reduced contributions to Bush. Later, the three-way race with Ross Perot hurt Bush more than it did Clinton because Perot attracted the votes of more Republicans than Democrats.

In November 1992, Bill Clinton won 43 percent of the popular vote, George H. W. Bush 38 percent, and Ross Perot 19 percent. In the Electoral College, Clinton won 370 votes to Bush's 138. Unlike the 1988 election, voters turned out in droves. For the first time in thirty years, voter turnout rose.

Adding to Bush's grief, two weeks later, he received news that his mother was dying. He and Doro flew to Greenwich to see her. Weeping at her bedside, Bush thought of all she had taught him about life. That evening, Dorothy Walker Bush died. She was ninety-one years old.

Bush's last days in office were busy ones. He sent an aid mission to Somalia, where civil unrest was causing starvation. He signed NAFTA with Mexico and Canada to lift tariffs from all goods traded among the three countries. Finally, to close the long-lasting investigation into the Iran-Contra scandal, he pardoned six men accused of taking part in it before their trials had even begun. The independent counsel conducting the investigation, Lawrence Walsh, condemned Bush's actions. Walsh and others believed that Bush was making sure that the trials did not reveal more details about his own role in the scandal.

Barbara Bush

Soon after Barbara Pierce married George Bush, she was asked, "How would you like to be First Lady?" Barbara Bush replied, "I'd like it." Then she added, "Because, you know, I'm going to be the First Lady sometime." About forty years later, her prophecy came true.

The third of four children, Barbara Pierce grew up in Rye, New York, a suburb of New York City. Her father, Marvin Pierce, was an executive at the McCall Publishing Company. An ancestor was Franklin Pierce, the fourteenth president of the United States.

Like her husband, she attended private schools and enjoyed sports. She did not finish college. Like most American women of her generation, Barbara Bush chose marriage and family as her career.

Her second son, Jeb, says she was a "supermom, serving as Cub Scout mother, carpool driver, and Sunday school teacher. Dad was the chief executive officer, but mother was the chief operating officer. We all reported to her. She did a good job of keeping the family intact."

When her husband entered politics in 1962, Barbara Bush stood by him. She campaigned for him every time he ran for office. She got to know Washington during Bush's two terms in Congress. She mastered diplomatic protocol when her husband served in the United Nations and in China. Her skills as a hostess eased her husband's rise in political life. By the time she became First Lady in 1988, Barbara Bush was a seasoned pro.

As the wife of the vice president and as First Lady, Barbara Bush focused on literacy as her special cause. "I chose literacy," she told Wellesley College graduates in a 1990 commencement speech, "because I honestly believe that if more people could read, write, and comprehend, we would be that much closer to solving so many of the problems plaguing our society."

In 1989 she founded the Barbara Bush Foundation for Family Literacy. This private charity gives grants to organizations that help adults and children to "learn and read together."

Her love of books led her to write four of her own. Two are stories narrated by Bush family dogs. *C. Fred's Story* tells of life in China and in the vice president's house from the point of view of their cocker spaniel. *Millie's Book* reports on the doings of their springer spaniel, whose six puppies amused White House visitors during Bush's presidency. These books raised over one million dollars for literacy. Since the Bushes left the White House, she has written two memoirs.

——————— ✧

Barbara Bush celebrates the release of Millie's Book *in September 1990.*

CHAPTER TEN

LOOKING FORWARD

*There is a life after the White House and both
of us are looking forward to it.*
—Barbara Bush, diary entry, summer 1990

Six months before leaving the White House, Bush drew a rosy picture of his retirement: "I'll be a very happy guy. I'll be opening the beans and the franks . . . Sunday nights," he wrote in his diary. "I'll be washing the dishes with Bar. I'll be going to bed early every once in a while; do something to help someone else; hold my grandchildren in my arms; look for the shellfish; take them fishing."

On January 20, 1993, the Bushes flew to Houston to make that dream come true. They planned to split their time between Texas and Maine. They lived in a rented house while they built a new home in Houston. In Maine they renovated Bush's mother's cottage to make plenty of room for visits from friends and family—especially their fourteen grandchildren.

A PRIVATE CITIZEN

Bush was eager to leave the political limelight. "I am out of the interview business," he wrote a friend in 1993. He kept a promise to his successor in the White House, President Bill Clinton, not to criticize or comment on what Clinton did.

The Bushes were far too used to hopping on planes to just stay home. In the years since he left the White House, Bush has taken many trips. With and without his wife, he has visited old friends and kept in touch with world leaders. The Bushes have also taken the opportunity to show the world to their grandchildren.

Bush, however, has not turned his back on public life. In September 1993, he returned to Washington for the signing of a peace accord between Israel and Palestine. He had played a major role in paving the way for the agreement. He stayed on to help Clinton persuade Congress to ratify NAFTA, which he had signed before leaving office.

He has worked as a senior adviser to the Carlyle Group investment firm. The Washington-based company employs a number of former government officials. They give advice and help the company make contacts with business opportunities around the world.

One of Bush's retirement goals was to help others. "I don't have myself cast as a big and important person," he wrote to a former press secretary. "I want to be a tiny point of light, hopefully a bright point of light."

To meet this goal, he has served on the Board of Trustees of the M. D. Anderson Cancer Center in Houston, contributed to leukemia research, and worked for the Crohn's and Colitis Foundation for research into these intestinal diseases. He was chairman of the Eisenhower Exchange Fellowship, which brings young people with leadership potential to the United States. He has been a member of the vestry, or governing committee, of his churches in Maine and Texas and serves on the board of the Episcopal Church Foundation.

A LIBRARY, A SCHOOL OF GOVERNMENT, AND BOOKS

The George Bush Presidential Library and Museum opened in November 1997 at Texas A&M University in College Station, Texas. The museum tells the story of Bush's life through photographs, documents, films, videos, and artifacts.

——————————— ◇ ———————————

From left: *Lady Bird Johnson, Jimmy and Rosalynn Carter, George and Barbara Bush, Bill and Hillary Clinton, Gerald and Betty Ford, and Nancy Reagan stand at the dedication of the George Bush Presidential Library and Museum on November 6, 1997, in College Station, Texas.*

The George Bush School of Government and Public Service opened the same year. The school prepares graduate students for careers devoted to helping others through public office, business, or nonprofit organizations. The two-year program leads to a master's degree. An inscription in the main hall quotes Bush: "Public service is a noble calling and we need men and women of character to believe in their communities, in their states, and in their country."

In the years since he left the White House, Bush has published two books. With his national security adviser, Brent Scowcroft, he wrote *A World Transformed*. The book focuses on the major world events during his presidency. It gives an inside look at his responses to the massacre at Tiananmen Square, the fall of the Berlin Wall, the end of the Soviet Union, and Saddam Hussein's invasion of Kuwait.

A second book, *All the Best, George Bush,* links together a selection of Bush's letters, diary entries, memos, and other writings. In it, matters of state share equal billing with family events. In the preface, he says that he published the book to show his values and what has motivated him in life. "It's all about heartbeat," he said.

RECENT ACTIVITIES

In recent years, Bush has agreed to several interviews. Since his son George W. Bush became president in 2001, everyone wants to know how he thinks his son is doing. Bush shows his pride in the political careers of his two sons, George W. and Jeb (governor of Florida), but he does not critique their actions.

George and Barbara Bush (top left) *read to schoolchildren*
in Bryan, Texas, in 2003.

——————— ✧ ———————

With his wife, Bush has supported the Boys and Girls Clubs of America. He has traveled with her on AmeriCares missions to bring aid to areas devastated by war or natural disasters. He also works with her on literacy projects. With former President Bill Clinton, he has led private fund-raising efforts to help victims of the 2004 tsunamis in Southeast Asia and Hurricane Katrina, which struck Alabama, Louisiana, and Mississippi in 2005.

APPRAISALS OF THE BUSH PRESIDENCY

"I hope history will show I did some things right," Bush wrote. A recent poll of historians and political scientists suggests that history will give him good marks for his "firm grasp of foreign policy." His handling of the Persian Gulf crisis, one assessment asserts, was "a major triumph."

Scholars often criticize Bush's handling of domestic issues. He put off dealing with economic problems too long, they say. He did not work well with Congress. Instead of forming bipartisan coalitions to write good laws, he used the veto to stop laws he didn't like. But Bush's domestic record is not all negative. Many praise him for the Americans with Disabilities Act, the Clean Air Act, and the savings and loan bailout.

A recent study points out that Bush's style was one of caution. He took one step at a time rather than try to make major changes. This worked well, but Bush was not good at letting people know what he was doing. Voters want to know their leader's goals, but Bush did not think what he called "the vision thing" was important.

The same study points out Bush's frequent use of secrecy by controlling the flow of information. Journalists covering military operations in Panama and the Persian Gulf, for example, faced tight restrictions on where they could go and to whom they could speak. He also kept information about many of his actions from Congress and U.S. citizens by issuing National Security Directives, which can be kept secret for security reasons. A number of these directives are still unavailable to the public. These secret orders, they argue, enabled him to get around the checks and balances among the three parts of the government provided in the Constitution. As a result, the president, not Congress, was making the law, and he left as his legacy widened powers of the U.S. presidency.

TIMELINE

1924 George Herbert Walker Bush is born on June 12 in Milton, Massachusetts.

1926 The Bush family settles in Greenwich, Connecticut.

1937 George enters Phillips Academy at Andover, Massachusetts.

1942 Bush graduates from Andover. He joins the navy on June 12.

1943 Bush earns his wings as the navy's youngest aviator on June 9.

1944 Bush serves on the USS *San Jacinto* in the Pacific. On September 2, his bomber is shot down during an attack on Chichi Jima in the Bonin Islands.

1945 Bush marries Barbara Pierce on January 6. He enters Yale University in New Haven, Connecticut, in September.

1946 George Walker Bush is born on July 6.

1948 Bush graduates from Yale. He goes to work in the oil business in Odessa, Texas.

1949 Bush moves to California. In December his daughter Robin is born.

1950 The Bushes move to Midland, Texas.

1951 Bush cofounds Bush-Overbey Oil Development.

1952 Bush's father, Prescott Bush, becomes a U.S. senator. George Bush works for Eisenhower's campaign for president.

1953 John Ellis (Jeb) Bush is born in February. Bush cofounds Zapata Petroleum Company in March. His daughter Robin dies of leukemia in October.

1954 Bush becomes cofounder and president of Zapata Offshore division of Zapata Petroleum.

1955   Neil Mallon Bush is born.

1956   Marvin Pierce Bush is born. Bush campaigns for the reelection of Eisenhower.

1959   Bush takes over Zapata Offshore. The Bushes move to Houston. Dorothy Walker (Doro) Bush is born.

1963   Bush is chosen chairman of the Republican Party in Harris County.

1964   Bush enters the race for senator from Texas. He wins the primary but loses the election to Democrat Ralph Yarborough.

1965   Bush decides to sell Zapata Offshore and run for Congress.

1966   Bush is elected to the U.S. House of Representatives from Texas's Seventh District.

1968   Bush is reelected to the House, unopposed.

1970   Bush runs for the Senate and loses to Lloyd Bentsen. In December President Richard Nixon appoints Bush ambassador to the United Nations.

1972   Prescott Bush dies in October. President Nixon asks Bush to become chairman of the Republican National Committee.

1974   President Gerald Ford names Bush chief of the U.S. Liaison Office in the People's Republic of China.

1975   Bush is appointed director of the Central Intelligence Agency.

1977   The Bushes leave Washington for Houston.

1979   Bush declares his candidacy for president of the United States.

1980   Bush loses to Ronald Reagan in the primaries. Reagan asks Bush to be his running mate.

1981   Bush is inaugurated vice president of the United States.

1985 Bush is inaugurated for his second term as U.S. vice president.

1986 Investigations into the Iran-Contra scandal begin.

1988 Bush is elected president of the United States.

1989 Bush signs the savings and loan bailout. He orders the invasion of Panama.

1990 Bush signs the Americans with Disabilities Act and the Clean Air Act. When Iraq invades Kuwait, Bush organizes an embargo of Iraq and a coalition to defend Saudi Arabia. A budget impasse leads to a three-day shutdown of the federal government.

1991 The Persian Gulf War begins January 16 and ends March 3. Bush nominates Clarence Thomas to the Supreme Court. Bush signs the Civil Rights Act.

1992 Bush loses the election to Governor Bill Clinton of Arkansas. Before leaving office, Bush sends U.S. troops to protect food aid to Somalia and signs the North American Free Trade Agreement (NAFTA). He closes investigation of the Iran-Contra scandal by pardoning the accused.

1993 The Bushes leave the White House for homes in Houston and Kennebunkport.

1998 Bush publishes *A World Transformed*, written with Brent Scowcroft, about the conclusion of the Cold War, changes in China, Desert Storm, and the collapse of the Soviet Union.

1999 Bush publishes *All the Best, George Bush: My Life in Letters and Other Writings*.

2005 President George W. Bush appoints Bush and former President Bill Clinton to raise money from private sources to aid victims of the tsunamis in Southeast Asia and Hurricane Katrina in Alabama, Louisiana, and Mississippi.

Source Notes

7 "Transcript of Bush Speech Accepting Presidential Nomination," *New York Times*, August 19, 1988, A14.

7 George Bush, *All the Best, George Bush: My Life in Letters and Other Writings* (New York: Scribner, 1999), 395.

7 Ibid.

7–8 "Transcript of Bush Speech."

8 George Bush, *All the Best*, 395.

9 Peggy Noonan, *What I Saw at the Revolution: A Political Life in the Reagan Era* (New York: Random House, 1990), 317.

9 John Robert Greene, American Presidency Series, *The Presidency of George Bush* (Lawrence: University Press of Kansas, 2000), 37.

10 Barry Bearak, "Team Player Bush: A Yearning to Serve," *Los Angeles Times*, November 22, 1987, 34.

11 Bearak, 34.

12 George Bush *Looking Forward,* with Victor Gold, (New York: Doubleday, 1987), 27.

13 Fitzhugh Green, *George Bush, an Intimate Portrait* (New York: Hippocrene Books, 1989), 17.

13 Herbert S. Parmet, *George Bush: The Life of a Lone Star Yankee* (New York: Scribner and Sons, 1997), 27.

13 George Bush, *Looking Forward*, 27.

13 Ibid, 29.

14 Ibid, 29.

14 Ibid, 29.

14 Ibid, 29.

15 Parmet, 38.

15 Ibid, 37.

15 Ibid, 40.

15–16 Ibid, 41.

17 Green, 25.

17 Ibid.

18 George Bush, *Looking Forward*, 30.

19 Ibid, 26.

19 Ibid, 119.

20 George Bush, *All the Best*, 59.

20 George Bush, *Looking Forward*, 30.

21 Joe Hyams, *Flight of the Avenger: George Bush at War* (San Diego: Harcourt Brace Jovanovich, 1991), 32.

22 Ibid, 40.

23 Ibid, 54.

24 Ibid, 83.

26 George Bush, *Looking Forward*, 36.

26 Hyams, 107.

26 Robert B. Stinnett, *George Bush: His World War II Years* (Washington, DC: Brassey's Inc., 1992), 161.

27 George Bush, *Looking Forward*, 38.

28 Hyams, 125.

28 George Bush, *Looking Forward*, 40.

29 "Lt. George Bush's Distinguished Flying Cross Citation," *Naval Historical Center Website*, http://www.history.navy.mil/faqs/faq10-2.htm

30 George Bush, *All the Best*, 62.

30 Parmet, 63.

30 George Bush, *Looking Forward*, 43.

31 Ibid, 44.

33 Ibid, 22.
34 Ibid, 46.
35 George Bush, *All the Best*, 68.
35 George Bush, *Looking Forward*, 56.
35 Ibid, 60.
35 Ibid, 60.
36 Bearak, 35.
36 George Bush, *Looking Forward*, 56.
36 Barbara Bush, *Barbara Bush, A Memoir* (New York: Charles Scribner's Sons, 1994), 38.
37 George Bush, *Looking Forward*, 69.
37 Childhood Leukemia Center, "Frequently Asked Questions," *Patient Centers*, http://www.patientcenters .com/leukemia/news/ leukfaq.html <January 2000>.
39 George Bush, *Looking Forward*, 83.
40 Parmet, 109.
40 Barbara Bush, 55.
40–41 Green, 73.
41 George Bush, *Looking Forward*, 85.
42 Parmet, 102.
42 George Bush, *All the Best*, 94.
43 Ibid, 95.
45 Ibid, 107.
45 George Bush, *Looking Forward*, 93.
47 Bearak, 36.
47 Bob Woodward and Walter Pincus, "A Public Life Courting the More Powerful," *Washington Post*, August 8, 1988, A8.
47 Barbara Bush, 78.
48 Woodward and Pincus, "A Public Life."
49 George Bush, *Looking Forward*, 108.

49 Ibid, 111.
50 George Bush, *All the Best*, 139.
51 Ibid, 152.
51 Ibid, 161.
52 Bearak, 36.
52 George Bush, *Looking Forward*, 121.
52 Bearak, 36.
53 Richard Ben Cramer, *What It Takes: The Way to the White House* (New York: Random House, 1992), 612.
54 George Bush, *All the Best*, 193.
54 George Bush, *Looking Forward*, 125.
55 George Bush, *All the Best*, 195.
55 George Bush, *Looking Forward*, 130.
55 George Bush, *All the Best*, 200.
57 George Bush, *Looking Forward*, 153.
57 George Bush, *All the Best*, 234.
57 George Bush, *Looking Forward*, 156.
58 Barbara Bush, 132.
58 John Ranelagh, *The Agency: The Rise and Decline of the CIA* (New York: Simon & Schuster, 1987), 632.
59 Bob Woodward and Walter Pincus, "At CIA, a Rebuilder 'Goes With the Flow,'" *Washington Post*, August 10, 1988, A8.
60 Bearak, 36.
60 George Bush, *All the Best*, 272.
62 Ibid, 276.
64 George Bush, *Looking Forward*, 187.
65 Bearak, 36.
65 Parmet, 226.
66 Roy Reed, "George Bush on the Move," *New York Times*

Magazine, February 10, 1980, p. 58.

66 George Bush, *All the Best*, 297.

66 Green, 182.

67 Barbara Bush, 154.

67 Green, 182.

68 George Bush, *All the Best*, 316.

68 Parmet, 246.

68 Ibid, 246.

70 George Bush, *Looking Forward*, 225.

70 Bearak, 37.

70 George Bush, *Looking Forward*, 233.

71 Green, 196.

72 George Bush and Brent Scowcroft, *A World Transformed* (New York: Knopf, 1998), 4.

72 George Bush, *All the Best*, 348.

73 David Hoffman, "A Politician Who Puts Personal Ties First," *Washington Post*, August 12, 1988, A10.

74 George Bush, *Looking Forward*, 251.

74 Parmet, 326.

74 Ibid, 309.

77 George Bush, *Public Papers of Presidents of the United States: George Bush* 1989–1993 (Washington, DC: Government Printing Office, 1990), 1:1.

77 Ibid.

77 Ibid, 1:2.

78 Ibid, 1:3.

78 George Bush, *All the Best*, 414.

80 Greene, 77.

80 Green, 84.

84 George Bush, *Public Papers,* 2:1,221.

85 Ibid, 2:1,114.

85–86 Ibid, 2:1,108.

86 Parmet, 473.

86 Ibid, 475.

87 Ibid, 483.

88 George Bush, *Public Papers,* 1:221.

91 George Bush, *All the Best,* 549.

92 Parmet, 36.

92 Green, 165.

93 George Bush Presidential Library and Museum website, "Text of Mrs. Bush's Remarks at Wellesley College Commencement," http://bushlibrary.tamu.edu/biosandphotos/commencementspeech.html (accessed May 25, 2006).

93 The Barbara Bush Foundation for Family Literacy, "Mission Statement," http://www.barbarabushfoundation.com/index.html. Updated April 30, 2004 (accessed May 25, 2006).

94 Barbara Bush, 361.

94 George Bush, *All the Best,* 563.

95 Ibid, 586.

96 Ibid, 589.

97 Bush School of Government and Public Service, "About Us," http://bush.tamu.edu/about%5Fus/ (accessed May 25, 2006).

97 George Bush, *All the Best,* 22.

98 Greene, 181.

98 William J. Ridings Jr. and Stuart B. McIver, *Rating the Presidents* (Secaucus, NJ: Carol Publishing Group, 1997), 271.

99 Thomas E. Cronin, "The George Bush Presidency," *Eyes on the President, George Bush,* ed. Leo E. Heagerty (Occidental, CA: Chronos Publishing, 1993), 6.

SELECTED BIBLIOGRAPHY

Barilleaux, Ryan J., and Mark J. Rozell. *Power and Prudence: The Presidency of George H. W. Bush.* College Station: Texas A&M University Press, 2004.

Bearak, Barry. "Team Player Bush: A Yearning to Serve." *Los Angeles Times,* November 22, 1987, 1, 34–37.

Bush, Barbara. *Barbara Bush: A Memoir.* New York: Charles Scribner's Sons, 1994.

Bush, George. *All the Best, George Bush: My Life in Letters and Other Writings.* New York: Scribner, 1999.

———. *Looking Forward.* with Victor Gold. New York: Doubleday, 1987.

———. *Public Papers of Presidents of the United States: George Bush 1989–1993.* 8 vols. Washington, DC: Government Printing Office, 1990.

Bush, George, and Brent Scowcroft. *A World Transformed.* New York: Alfred Knopf, 1998.

Cramer, Richard Ben. *What It Takes: The Way to the White House.* New York: Random House, 1992.

Freedman, Lawrence, and Efraim Karsh. *The Gulf Conflict 1990–1991: Diplomacy and War in the New World Order.* Princeton, NJ: Princeton University Press, 1993.

Green, Fitzhugh. *George Bush, an Intimate Portrait.* New York: Hippocrene Books, 1989.

Greene, John Robert. *The Presidency of George Bush.* American Presidency series. Lawrence: University Press of Kansas, 2000.

Heagerty, Leo E., ed. *Eyes on the President, George Bush: History in Essays and Cartoons.* Occidental, CA: Chronos Publishing, 1993.

Hess, Gary R. *Presidential Decisions for War: Korea, Vietnam, and the Persian Gulf.* Baltimore: Johns Hopkins University Press, 2001.

Hyams, Joe. *Flight of the Avenger: George Bush at War.* San Diego: Harcourt Brace Jovanovich, 1991.

Kornbluh, Peter, and Malcolm Berne. *The Iran-Contra Scandal: The Declassified History, A National Security Archive Documents Reader.* New York: New Press, 1993.

McGrath, Jim, ed. *Heartbeat: George Bush in his Own Words.* New York: Scribner, 2001.

Mervin, David. *George Bush and the Guardianship Presidency.* New York: St. Martin's Press, 1996.

Morley, Jefferson. "Bush and the Blacks: An Unknown Story." *New York Review of Books,* January 16, 1992, 19–26.

Noonan, Peggy. *What I Saw at the Revolution: A Political Life in the Reagan Era.* New York: Random House, 1990.

Parmet, Herbert S. *George Bush: The Life of a Lone Star Yankee.* New York: Scribner and Sons, 1997.

Phillips, Kevin. *American Dynasty: Aristocracy, Fortune, and the Politics of Deceit in the House of Bush.* New York: Viking, 2004.

Ranelagh, John. *The Agency: The Rise and Decline of the CIA.* New York: Simon & Schuster, 1987.

———. *CIA, a History.* London: BBC Books, 1992.

Reed, Roy. "George Bush on the Move." *New York Times Magazine,* February 10, 1980, 20–23, 54–58, 73.

Ridings, William J., Jr., and Stuart B. McIver. *Rating the Presidents.* Secaucus, NJ: Carol Publishing Group, 1997.

Rothenberg, Randall. "In Search of George Bush." *New York Times Magazine,* March 6, 1988, 29–30, 44–49, 61.

Stinnett, Robert B. *George Bush: His World War II Years.* Washington, DC: Brassey's Inc., 1992.

Unger, Craig. *House of Bush, House of Saud: The Secret Relationship between the World's Two Most Powerful Dynasties.* New York: Scribner, 2004.

Waas, Murray, and Craig Unger. "In the Loop: Bush's Secret Mission." *New Yorker,* November 2, 1992, 64–83.

Walsh, Lawrence E. *Iran-Contra, the Final Report.* New York: Times Books, 1994.

Woodward, Bob. *Shadow: Five Presidents and the Legacy of Watergate.* New York: Simon & Schuster, 1999.

Woodward, Bob, Walter Pincus, and David Hoffman. "George Bush: Man and Politician." *Washington Post,* August 7, 1988–August 12, 1988.

FURTHER READING AND WEBSITES

American Presidents
http://www.americanpresident.org/history/georgebush
This site gives brief biographies of George H. W. and Barbara Pierce Bush, lists of his cabinet and staff, and the main events of his years in office.

Bush, Barbara. *C. Fred's Story.* Garden City, NY: Doubleday, 1984.

Crothers, Lane, and Nancy S. Lind. *Presidents from Reagan through Clinton, 1981–2001: Debating the Issues through Pro and Con Documents.* Westwood, CT: Greenwood Press, 2002.

George Bush Presidential Library and Museum
http://bushlibrary.tamu.edu
This website offers biographical information about George H. W. and Barbara Pierce Bush, tours of the museum, and access to public papers from the Bush administration.

Gottfried, Ted. *The Cold War.* Minneapolis: Twenty-First Century Books, 2003.

Márquez, Herón. *George W. Bush.* Minneapolis: Twenty-First Century Books, 2007.

Marrin, Albert. *Victory in the Pacific.* New York: Atheneum, 1983.

Naval Historical Center, Frequently Asked Questions
http://www.history.navy.mil/faqs/faq10-1.htm
The website of the Department of the Navy answers questions about George Bush's naval career during World War II.

Schuman, Michael A. *George H. W. Bush.* Hillside, NJ: Enslow Publishers, 2002.

Sherman, Josepha. *The Cold War.* Minneapolis: Twenty-First Century Books, 2004.

Sullivan, George. *Journalists at Risk: Reporting America's Wars.* Minneapolis: Twenty-First Century Books, 2006.

The White House
http://www.whitehouse.gov/history/presidents/gb41.html
The White House's website includes brief biographies of George H. W. Bush and Barbara Pierce Bush.

Zeinert, Karen, and Mary Miller. *The Brave Women of the Gulf Wars: Operation Desert Storm and Operation Iraqi Freedom.* Minneapolis: Twenty-First Century Books, 2006.

Zwier, Larry, and Matthew Weltig. *The Persian Gulf and Iraqi Wars.* Minneapolis: Twenty-First Century Books, 2005.

INDEX

ABOUT THE AUTHOR

Diana Childress writes about history, archaeology, art, and science for children's magazines and textbooks. She is the author of several books for young people, including *Prehistoric People of North America, Chaucer's England,* and *The War of 1812.* Originally from Houston, Texas, Childress grew up in Mexico City and lives in New York City. She has a doctorate in English literature. She has taught English at the college level and has also worked as a school librarian.

◇

PHOTO ACKNOWLEDGMENTS

The images in this book are used with the permission of: The White House, pp. 1, 7, 10, 20, 30, 40, 48, 60, 68, 77, 84, 94; George Bush Presidential Library, pp. 2, 11, 12, 15, 16, 18, 21, 22, 29, 31, 34, 38, 41, 43, 44, 52, 56, 64, 72, 75, 76, 79, 85, 87, 88, 90, 93, 96, 98; © Philip Gould/CORBIS, p. 6; © Shepard Sherbell/CORBIS SABA, p. 9; © CORBIS, p. 27; © Rykoff Collection/CORBIS, p. 33; © Bettmann/CORBIS, pp. 46, 63; © Ron Sachs/Corbis NY/CNP/CORBIS, p. 49; © Wally McNamee/CORBIS, p. 54; AP/Wide World Photos, pp. 58, 69; © Todd Strand/Independent Picture Service, p. 67; © Keystone/Getty Images, p. 82.

Cover: © MPI/Getty Images